Overdraft

Overdraft
Saving the Indian Saver

URJIT PATEL

HARPER BUSINESS
An Imprint of HarperCollins *Publishers*

First published in hardback in India in 2020 by Harper Business
An imprint of HarperCollins *Publishers*
A-75, Sector 57, Noida, Uttar Pradesh 201301, India
www.harpercollins.co.in

2 4 6 8 10 9 7 5 3 1

Copyright © Urjit R. Patel 2020

P-ISBN: 978-93-5357-914-2
E-ISBN: 978-93-5357-915-9

The views and opinions expressed in this book are the author's own and the facts are as reported by him, and the publishers are not in any way liable for the same.

Urjit R. Patel asserts the moral right
to be identified as the author of this work.

All rights reserved. No part of this publication may be reproduced, stored in a retrieval system, or transmitted, in any form or by any means, electronic, mechanical, photocopying, recording or otherwise, without the prior permission of the publishers.

Typeset in 12/16 Adobe Garamond at
Manipal Technologies Limited, Manipal

Printed and bound at
Manipal Technologies Limited, Manipal

For the Indian saver

CONTENTS

List of Abbreviations ix

Preface xiii

A: THE BACKDROP

1. Overview 3
2. Plenty of Blame to Go Around 13
3. A Tale of Two Sectors 24

B: CLEANSING THE AUGEAN STABLES

4. The First 4Rs: Recognize the Reality, Record, Report, Recovery 35
5. The 5th R: Resolution 41
6. The 6th R: Reinforced Resolution – Cutting the Gordian Knot 47

7.	The 7th R: Recapitalization and the Fiscal Dimension	53
8.	The 8th R: Reset and Ring-Fence to Cement the Change	60
9.	The Empire Strikes Back	70
10.	Outcomes and Implications of the Rs	84
11.	The 9th R: Reform – Gone AWOL	93

C: BITS AND PIECES

12.	Agriculture Credit	111
13.	Preventive Vigilance	124
14.	Regulation and Policies in a World of Excessive Financialization	135
15.	Remarks at the Meghnad Desai Academy of Economics	147
16.	Conclusions and the Trilemma	152

D: APPENDICES

Appendix 1: *Aggravated* Moral Hazard in the Indian Financial System	163
Appendix 2: Ping-pong: Timeline of a Litigation (NCLT, NCLAT and the SC)	181
Index	185
About the Author	195

LIST OF ABBREVIATIONS

AE	Advanced Economy
AMH	Aggravated Moral Hazard
AQR	Asset Quality Review
BCP	Basel Core Principles
BR Act	Banking Regulation Act, 1949
BRICS	Brazil, Russia, India, China, South Africa
CAG	Comptroller and Auditor General
CAR	Capital Adequacy Ratio
CBI	Central Bureau of Investigation
CFM	Capital Flow Management
CIRP	Corporate Insolvency Resolution Process

LIST OF ABBREVIATIONS

CP	Core Principle
CRAR	Capital to Risk (weighted) Assets Ratio
CRILC	Central Repository of Information on Large Credits
CVC	Central Vigilance Commission
DRT	Debt Recovery Tribunal
EBITDA	Earnings Before Interest, Taxes, Depreciation and Amortization
EMEs	Emerging Market Economies
FA	Financial Accelerator
FII	Foreign Institutional Investor
FLC	Financial Leverage Coefficient
FRBM	Fiscal Responsibility and Budget Management
FRDI	Financial Resolution and Deposit Insurance
FSAP	Financial Sector Assessment Programme
FSDP	Financial Stability and Development Council
FSP	Financial Service Provider
FSSA	Financial System Stability Assessment
FSR	Financial Stability Report, Reserve Bank of India
GB(s)	Government Bank(s) (in which the government is the majority shareholder)
GDP	Gross Domestic Product
GFSN	Global Financial Safety Net
GNPA(s)	Gross Non-Performing Asset(s)

List of Abbreviations

GoI	Government of India
GSDP	Gross State Domestic Product
HC	High Court
HFC	Housing Finance Company
IAC	Internal Advisory Committee
IBBI	Insolvency and Bankruptcy Board of India
IBC	Insolvency and Bankruptcy Code, 2016
ICA	Inter-creditor Agreement
IFRS	International Financial Reporting Standards
IMF	International Monetary Fund
Ind AS	Indian Accounting Standards
JLF	Joint Lenders' Forum
LIC	Life Insurance Corporation
LTV	Loan to Value
MPM	Macro-Prudential Measure
MSME	Micro, Small, Medium Enterprise
NBFC	Non-Banking Financial Company
NCLAT	National Company Law Appellate Tribunal
NCLT	National Company Law Tribunal
NIM	Net Interest Margin
NPA(s)	Non-Performing Asset(s)
OC	Overseeing Committee
PB(s)	Private Bank(s)
PCA	Prompt Corrective Action
PCR	Provision Coverage Ratio

LIST OF ABBREVIATIONS

RBI	Reserve Bank of India
RDDBFI	Recovery of Debts Due to Banks and Financial Institutions Act, 1993
RoA	Return on Assets
RoE	Return on Equity
SARFAESI	Securitisation and Reconstruction of Financial Assets and Enforcement of Security Interest Act, 2002
SBI	State Bank of India
SC	Supreme Court
SCB	Scheduled Commercial Bank
SDR	Strategic Debt Restructuring Mechanism
S4A	Sustainable Structuring of Stressed Assets
SIB	Systemically Important Bank
SIFI	Systemically Important Financial Institution
SMA	Special Mention Accounts
SPARC	Supervisory Programme for Assessment of Risk and Capital
SPPAB	Special Purpose Power Assets Bank
TBTF	Too Big to Fail
WB	World Bank

PREFACE

I HAVE BEEN IN the news; while it lasted, the contretemps made good theatre. It ended when I stepped down. The theatre of eminences has been going on for centuries and will continue for many more; eventually, everyone is forgotten. I do not wish to write about these passing matters. But there are some issues of economic outlook and policy that are important for our nation's destiny; it is essential to address them correctly. I have written this book to share my approach to them with my fellow citizens. I may be right or wrong; you may agree or disagree with me. What matters is that the correct solution should emerge out of public debate – on the issues, not the personalities. Hence, this book. If it contributes towards pointing our economy in the

PREFACE

right direction, it will have served its purpose. In the meantime, enjoy the drama of monetary policy.

A book is a good opportunity to acknowledge debts by expressing gratitude to mentors, teachers, colleagues and fellow travellers. This project was initiated and concluded with the help and encouragement of Ashok V. Desai, Arvind Panagariya, Jalpa Mapara, Rahool Pai-Panandiker, and Krishan Chopra of HarperCollins. The kernel for the book was drawn from speaking engagements in 2019 at Stanford (the 19th Annual Conference on Indian Economic Policy); University of California, Santa Cruz (seminar in the Department of Economics); Siena (Santa Colomba Conference); Yale (Wilbur Cross Medal oration in the Department of Economics); and Ahmedabad University (conference on '50 Years of Bank Nationalization: Indian Banking at Crossroads').

Some of the content resonates with the knowledge and mode of thinking that I was fortunate enough to imbibe from Willem H. Buiter, T.N. Srinivasan, Kenneth Kletzer, John Vickers, Vijay Kelkar, Sudhir Mulji and Deena Khatkhate. Deepak Lal was the first source of gainful employment in 1987; we also wrote a paper together.

Over many years, numerous friends and former colleagues gave support, professional and personal: I.G. Patel, Rajendra Pattni, Deepak Haria, Dan Pillay, Govinda Rao, Pratap Bhanu Mehta, Tushar Patel, M.G. Bhide, Makarand Dehejia, Chetan Ahya, Jagdish Bhagwati, Meghnad Desai, Yoginder Alagh, P.J. Nayak, Sajjid Chinoy, Raaj Sah, Girish Modi, Anjini Kochar, Flavio Delbono, Plutarchos Sakellaris, Jaydev Raja, Suman Bery,

Preface

Peter Sanfey, Pankaj Chandra, Suresh Mathur, Sandeep Dave, Anand Srinivasan, Bahram Vakil, Rajiv Desai, Nachiket Mor, Janmejaya Sinha and Vivek Dehejia.

Eswar Prasad, Ratna Sahay, Stephen Fries, Chandrakant Patel, Gopi Arora (IMF); Narendra Jadhav, R.K. Das, Viral Acharya, Bhupal Singh, Michael Patra, Anand Sinha, N.S. Vishwanathan, R. Gandhi, Malvika Sinha, G. Padmanabhan, B. Mahapatra, Yashpal Charan, Vaibhav Chaturvedi, Mridul Sagar, C. Rangarajan (RBI); Montek Singh Ahluwalia, N.K. Singh, Madhusudhan Prasad, Shankar Acharya, Arvind Virmani, Arvind Mayaram, Umesh Gupta, D.K. Mittal, Rajiv Mehrishi, Anjuly Chib Duggal, Ajay Tyagi, Tapan Ray, P.K. Mishra (Government of India); Mukesh Ambani, P.M.S. Prasad, Atul Chandra, Anil Dhar (Reliance Industries Limited); Deepak Parekh and Nasser Munjee (IDFC Limited).

I owe much to co-authors over the years, including Pradeep Srivastava, Vijay Joshi, Partha Mukhopadhyay, Saugata Bhattacharya, Amartya Lahiri, Srikumar Tadimalla, Nirmal Mohanty, Sunaina Kilachand, Devesh Kapur and Gangadhar Darbha.

Finally, I have to thank my mother, who must now be relieved. For the past few months she has endured, without complaint, my untidy work environment, taking up a disproportionate part of the flat.

A: THE BACKDROP

1

OVERVIEW

THE CREDIT MARKET IN India is prone to perilous setbacks, with the extant prolonged non-performing asset shock being the latest one. At the heart of the subject is the increasing risk, in effect, due to the failure, over decades, to arrest a creeping *banking sector-fiscalization*;[1] ownership of banks as a means for day-to-day macroeconomic management rather than primarily for efficient intermediation between savers and borrowers.[2]

---

1 Possibly since bank nationalization, but certainly in more recent decades.
2 These arguments, and others throughout the book, were first made in my presentation 'The Cul-de-sac in Indian Banking: A Dominant Government Sector, Limited Fiscal Space and

Indian finance ministers, somewhat unusually as compared to colleagues elsewhere, declare 'credit budgets' on behalf of banks in the annual finance speech; state chief ministers, for their part, announce quinquennial write-offs; in 2008, in the lead-up to elections in the following year, the Union government did both simultaneously! How we got here feels like a case of an Overton window in India's political economy, where 'gradual shifts over time make [previously] abnormal situations feel normal to anyone watching on'.[3] An inexorable upshot in such cases is that the financial burden on the national balance sheet snowballs and policy contradictions catch up (Chapters 7 and 16).

A positive outcome of successfully overcoming the current challenge would be a low-hanging opportunity to boost growth by putting moribund capital stock to work. The Indian financial ecosystem has been dominated by the official sector for much of the last half-century. The involvement is manifest through three broad channels: (i) unfettered ownership of numerous intermediaries; (ii) mobilization of resources; and (iii) policy prescriptions on credit.[4] These encompass marshalling of financial

---

Independent Regulation (Is There an "Impossible Trilemma"?)', keynote address at the 19th Annual Conference on Indian Economic Policy, Stanford University, 4 June 2019.

3 I came across this phrase in the context of the Overton window in Miguel Delaney, 'How Modern Football Became Broken Beyond Repair', *Independent*, 12 February 2020.

4 The pathological implications for transmission of monetary policy in an environment of endemic distortions have been worked out in detail in Amartya Lahiri and Urjit Patel, 'Challenges of Effective

Overview

savings and its utilization for investment and working capital. The government's instrumentality is both direct and through those of the entities it owns, as well as indirect, owing to statutory restrictions and social lending requirements.

Even after three decades of banking sector reforms, including entry of private banks, state-sponsored credit creation retains a majority share. Competition in the system has increased, but the large presence of government institutions in all segments – India and China are outliers amongst large economies in this respect – has meant that they still continue to be, in a manner of speaking, 'Stackelberg leaders' (Buiter and Patel [2006]).[5][6][7] The public ownership creates an environment where market discipline is perceptibly weak (Chapter 3), and where the regulator's remit is circumscribed (Chapter 11). Over decades, investment

---

Monetary Policy in Emerging Economies', in *Monetary Policy in India: A Modern Macroeconomic Perspective*, ed. Chetan Ghate and Kenneth M. Kletzer, Springer, 2016.

5 'Excessive Budget Deficits, a Government-Abused Financial System, and Fiscal Rules', *India Policy Forum* Vol. 2, Brookings Institution-NCAER, 2006, pp. 1–54.

6 In the sense that even the private and foreign banks continue to retain high lending rates and thereby maintain higher operating margins than the government-owned banks.

7 Also see Urjit Patel, 'Role of State-owned Financial Institutions in India: Should the Government "Do" or "Lead"?' in *The Future of State-owned Financial Institutions*, The Brookings Institution, ed. Gerard Caprio, Jonathan Fiechter, Robert Litan and Michael Pomerleano, Washington, DC, 2004.

entities, insurers, financial institutions and non-banking financial companies have been used to support vague (and extraneous) objectives – underwriting the government's disinvestment targets, preserving employment in public enterprises, contributing assistance to states based on the political clout of the representatives, intermittently providing artificial support to stock markets, and occasionally overt lapses in due diligence.[8]

The persisting management control of a large section of intermediaries by the sovereign engenders an irresistible temptation to increase the *density* of government participation in the financial sector by the growing use of a variety of practices (Bhattacharya and Patel [2002]; Bhattacharya and Patel [2005]).[9] A prominent reason is attempts by the government to boost public expenditure – through direct spending and indirectly through lenders – partially to counter low private investment. Correctly measured, Indian general government fiscal deficits are, year after year, rarely below 6.5

---

8 The Tinbergen principle is violated with impunity. The objectives unsurprisingly exceed the number of instruments, which leads to confused design.

9 Saugata Bhattacharya and Urjit Patel, 'Financial Intermediation in India: A Case of Aggravated Moral Hazard?', Working Paper No. 145, Stanford Centre for International Development (SCID), May 2002; Saugata Bhattacharya and Urjit Patel, 'Refrom Strategies in the Indian Financial Sector', in India's and China's Recent Experience with Reform and Growth, ed. Wanda Tseng and David Cowen, Basingstoke, U.K.: Palgrave Macmillan, 2005.

per cent of GDP – invariably amongst the highest in the G20. Moreover, the Public Sector Borrowing Requirement is usually 1-2 percentage points of GDP higher than the quantum that governments borrow directly. Normally and conceptually, fiscal stance can be differentiated as tight, neutral, accommodative and expansionary; in India, it is rarely anything other than *loose* and *very loose*. Regardless of where the country stands in the economic cycle, the fiscal tap is hardly ever restrained, that is, fiscal firepower is never kept in reserve for counter-cyclical impetus. In fact, matters are such that the payment risk for subsidy recipients, and for vendors to governments, is pro-cyclical; the current cycle is a case in point where, with faltering growth, the government's reputation as a timely paymaster, reportedly even for something as basic and as fundamental as statutory contributions and revenue share of states, has suffered. The economic slowdown will accentuate the drift.

As successive governments have found their capacity for further fiscal expansion becoming constrained, it has used the banks that it owns to fire up and pump-prime the economy; hence the term banking sector-fiscalization. We have been in the realm of political credit cycles for at least the last decade or so:

- Drum-beating higher credit growth to impart stimulus for growth and, concomitantly, job creation (Chapter 2). Even as the sector grapples with non-performing assets (NPAs), the government directed its banks[10] in October 2019 to extend credit in 250 districts to boost consumption.[11]

- Farm loan waivers that are redistributive in nature from taxpayers to borrowers (Chapter 12).
- Backward-looking prudential norms; inertia in adjusting risk weights on loans by the regulator (Chapter 2).

In this scenario, the normal mechanisms that mitigate moral hazard in agency situations are greatly weakened.[12] First, public ownership reduces the (risk-adjusted profit-maximizing) incentive for requiring optimal pure risk capital from borrowers

---

10 Banks owned by the sovereign are regulated by the Government of India under the Banking Companies (Acquisition and Transfer of Undertakings) Act, 1970; the Bank Nationalization Act, 1980; and the State Bank of India Act, 1955. Throughout the book, I collectively refer to all these banks as government banks (GBs).

11 The government on 3 December 2019 claimed – one presumes to highlight the success of its public exhortation – that ₹4.9 trillion had been disbursed in October and November. In comparison, the RBI's data, which is released every fortnight, suggested expansion of ₹584 billion (*Mint*, 16 December 2019, p.1).

12 These mechanisms were first elucidated in Saugata Bhattacharya and Urjit Patel, 'Financial Intermediation in India: A Case of Aggravated Moral Hazard?', Working Paper No. 145, Stanford Centre for International Development (SCID), May 2002; and Urjit Patel and Saugata Bhattacharya, 'The Financial Leverage Coefficient: Macroeconomic Implications of Government Involvement in Intermediation', Working Paper No. 157, Stanford Centre for International Development (SCID), October 2002.

Overview

– both the absolute levels and the effectiveness of co-financing decline (Chapter 4). The use of intermediaries by the government as quasi-fiscal instruments, with diversion of financing for non-commercial purposes, reinforces the decline in the quality of assets. Secondly, the absence of effective and time-bound bankruptcy procedures force intermediaries to roll over existing sub-standard debt or convert them into equity, thereby continually building up the riskiness of their asset portfolio and further diluting the (already weakened) notional leverage norms. Beyond a point the practice, in effect, morphs into a fraud in some instances, which comes to light years later (Chapters 3 and 11). Thirdly, a virtual certainty of sustained bailouts by the government replaces a policy of 'constructive ambiguity' (Mishkin, 1999)[13] with one of 'destructive unambiguity'. Fourthly, there is a higher regulatory forbearance for bank closure, given their public sector ownership. The resulting political economy of financial intermediation with the aforementioned characteristics leads to *aggravated* moral hazard (AMH). Inevitably, at some point, *self-correcting* processes – even the modest ones – stall. One can reasonably hypothesize that non-performing-asset–induced (financial) shocks have amplified the structural weakness in the Indian economy, with concomitant *lengthy* growth repercussions; this is elucidated and formally laid out in Appendix 1.[14]

---

13 Mishkin, F.S., 'Financial Market Reform', Mimeo., Columbia University, 1999.

14 There is *hysteresis*, so even when the shock is (partially) reversed, adverse consequences persist.

Banking is a business almost wholly conducted with other people's money, mostly those who place their savings as deposits; pure equity of those who own a bank can be even lower than 5.5 per cent of risk-weighted assets. Banking regulation is needed because, inter alia, there are externalities. I have worked in the private sector for almost half of my working life. For the first time, credit-worthy (corporate) borrowers are feeling the effect of non-performing assets (NPAs) that banks have to sustain on their balance sheets. There are two aspects around this issue:

1. Banks have to hold buffers in the capital structure to bear losses. All borrowers to some extent have to (indirectly) shoulder the 'carry cost' of distressed assets and, increasingly, frauds, through higher margins on their loans.
2. The uncertainty and lags around the resolution/liquidation process has meant that a (*recovery*) risk premium is added to the borrowing margin of *all* borrowers, including those who are diligently servicing their debt.

Over the period 2019 up to early 2020, although policy rates were cut by 135 basis points over eleven months, less than one-half have been transmitted for fresh loans.[15] It would seem that downward-sticky deposit rates are interacting with the NPA overhang. Even if deposit rates are relatively rigid, banks could cut

---

15 The transmission percentages were much higher (70 per cent) during the 2015 rate-cutting cycle when policy rates were cut by 125 basis points over nine months. In January 2020, lending rates for fresh loans actually went up by 7 basis points.

Overview

lending rates and work with lower net interest margins; however, their ability to do so has been impaired by the provisioning costs that they are incurring.

From 2014 onwards the regulator, the Reserve Bank of India (RBI), and the government have sought to work towards addressing the scourge of large NPAs – the thrust on transparency meant that the unveiled figure tripled to ₹10.4 trillion by 2018 – in a consistent manner (Chapters 4, 5, 6, 7 and 8). The overall path can be christened, in short, as the '9R' strategy, implemented in distinct steps; the 9Rs Chart is a snapshot to whet the reader's appetite. The task is the most intractable in the last three decades, not only because of the size, but also because the responses to it (the best there are, probably), while starting with great promise, are shedding traction (Chapter 9). Is there the possibility of no more bullets left? A critical public policy choice is playing out in India. There is a trilemma or cul-de-sac at the conjuncture of a dominant government sector, limited fiscal space and independent regulation. If it is an 'impossible trilemma', as it increasingly seems to be, something has to give way (Chapters 7 and 16).

The check and cross marks (with/out fractions), at the bottom of the 9Rs Chart are my shorthand combined assessment of: (i) the extent to which measures have been implemented in letter and spirit; (ii) the degree of regulatory and policy rollback; and (iii) how each of the 9 Rs has worked out in relation to the objective. For instance, while the 4th R was executed and did run its course, the outcome was pretty much nil, hence '×'.

OVERDRAFT

Chart 1.1: The 9Rs

Step 1 (First 4 Rs)				Step 2 (5th R)	Step 3 (6th R and 7th R)		Step 4 (8th R)	Step 5 (9th R – Reform) AWOL
Led to stark increase in NPAs as banks recognized issue.				Failed largely due to agency & moral hazard problems of not resolving NPAs when sector is majorly government-owned.	Aimed to legally enforce 5th R and Recapitalization commitment.		Cementing the change	Aimed at restoring faith in GBs.
Recognize (by banks, regulator, government) Information aggregation under CRILC started in June 2014.	**Record** (started in 2014-2015) Undertake AQR.	**Report** (started in 2015-2016)	**Recovery** under RBI's restructuring schemes ('alphabet soup') 2015/16.	**Resolution** under IBC 2016. RBI establishes Enforcement Department, distinct from Supervision and Regulation, in April 2017; an attempt to break the institutional 'Stockholm Syndrome'.	**Reinforced** regulation by RBI based on new statutory powers June 2017 onwards. Directions to banks on large mature NPAs.	**Recapitalization** 2015-2019; large quantum in 2018 and 2019.	**Reset & Ring Fence** • 12 February circular for defaults put an end to 'alphabet soup' of 'extend & pretend' schemes. • Banks put within PCA guardrails.	**Reform:** • Virtually missing. • Commitment to PCA cut short. • Routinely, senior positions in GBs have been vacant; board seats were unfilled. • Dual regulation of GBs by RBI and government not addressed.
3/4 ✓	✓	3/4 ✓	✗	1/2 ✓	1/2 ✓	1/2 ✓	1/4 ✓	✗

2

PLENTY OF BLAME TO GO AROUND

Pre-2014: All Hands on Deck for Stimulating the Economy

For most episodes of serious NPA build-up, including earlier ones in India, the dominant antecedent is *excessive* lending and borrowing; it is not surprising that in the decade since 2009/10, the bank credit–GDP ratio peaked in 2013/14.[1] (If we include corporate bonds outstanding, credit from non-banking financial companies [NBFCs], housing finance companies [HFCs] and cooperative banks, the augmented financial resources/GDP ratio

---

1 RBI Annual Report (2017/18) and RBI Annual Report (2018/19).

for 2018/19 is around an estimated 85 per cent.) Secondly, the asymmetry of information between the regulator and lenders, which is why the supervisor is almost always too late, is inevitably a critical ingredient. Thirdly, policymakers and regulators convince themselves, when the credit cycle is motoring along, that 'this time it is different' so there is no need to judiciously apply brakes – take away the 'punch bowl' or, at the least, dilute it. The present mountain of bad debt in India is no exception.

Among major economies, India is in the company of Russia and Italy in terms of asset quality as well as other key banking ratios like net non-performing assets (NPAs), provision coverage ratio (PCR), etc. (see Charts 2.1 and 2.2). Not surprisingly, a negative risk perception emerged.

The lending cycle/asset build-up started in the mid-2000s and even through the global financial crisis, we kept lending channels wide open – at a growth rate of about 17 per cent (in non-food credit) as late as 2011/12 – based on ambitious projections of debt-servicing capacity underpinned by an *assumption* of 8–8.5 per cent annual growth over a long period. Project execution would, in turn, have assumed minimal glitches or hold-ups. There was a (systemic) failure to maintain balanced credit expansion; non-food credit growth *annually* over 2006/07–2011/12 was 20 per cent versus the real GDP growth rate of around 7 per cent per annum.

> The reasons for the growth in the NPAs are also not far to seek. [The] bank debt fuelled the rise in corporate leverage steadily from 2005 to 2011.... Do we call this irrational

Plenty of Blame to Go Around

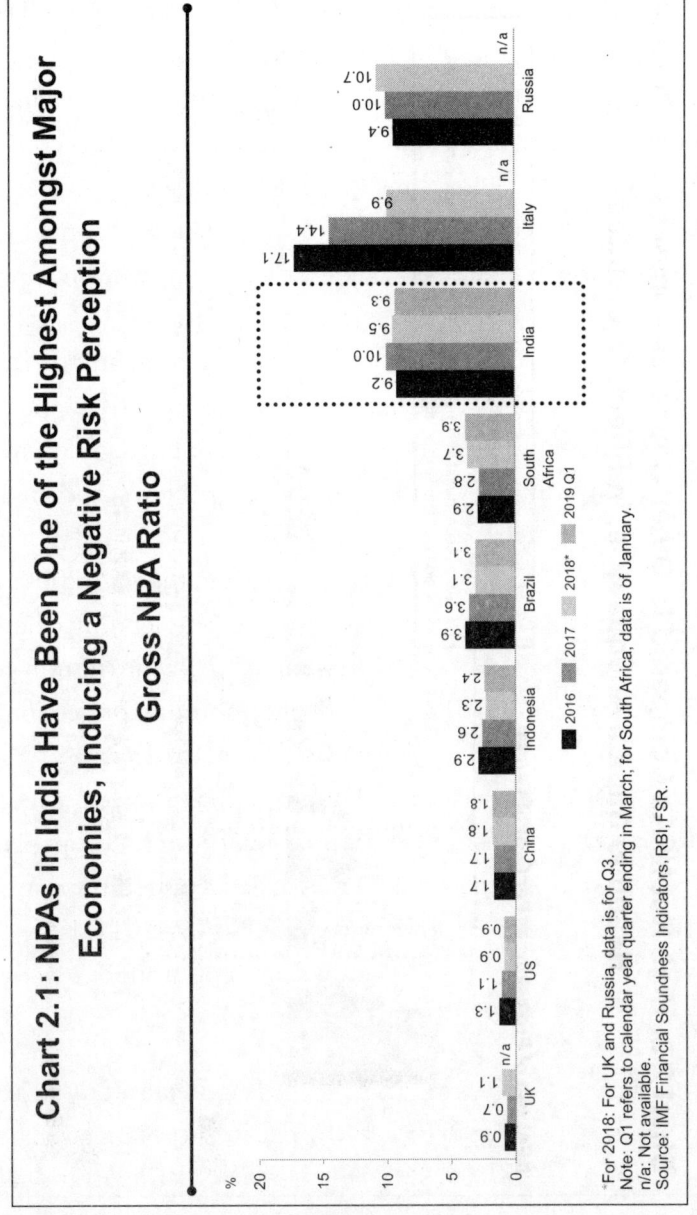

Chart 2.1: NPAs in India Have Been One of the Highest Amongst Major Economies, Inducing a Negative Risk Perception

*For 2018: For UK and Russia, data is for Q3.
Note: Q1 refers to calendar year quarter ending in March; for South Africa, data is of January.
n/a: Not available.
Source: IMF Financial Soundness Indicators, RBI, FSR.

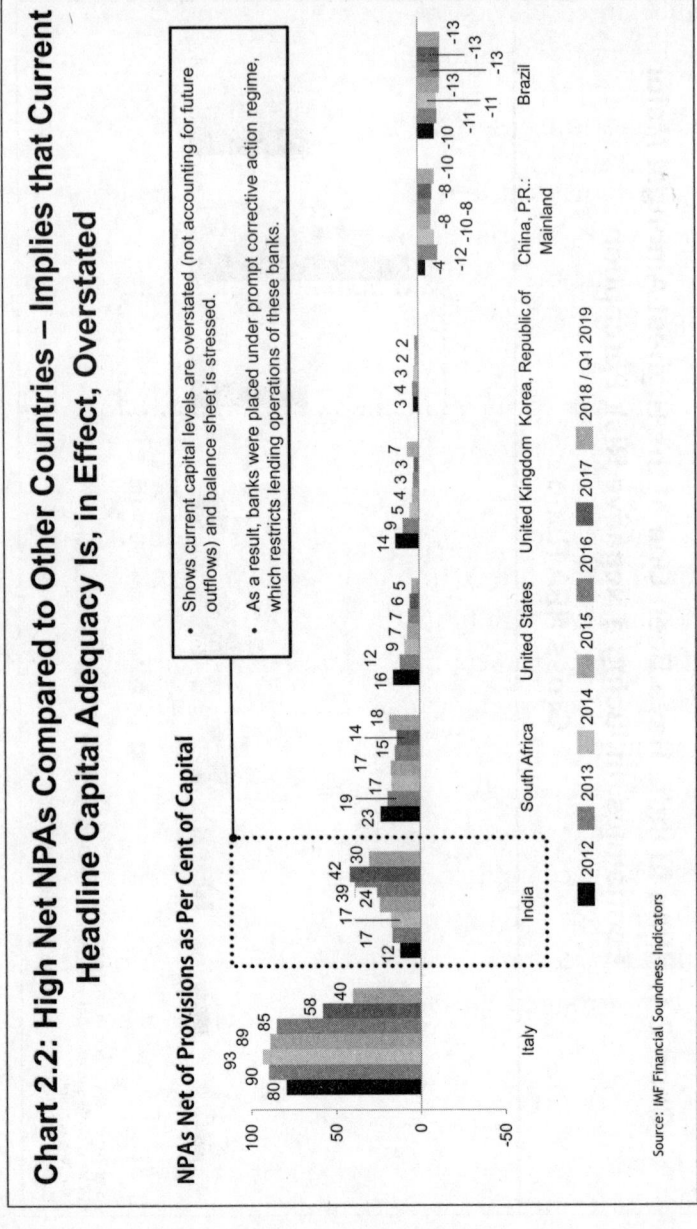

exuberance? Obviously, an overly leveraged business is more sensitive to turbulence (Vishwanathan [2016]).[2]

The Stakeholders

The government was not risk-managing from a macro-financial perspective. It, instead, encouraged government banks (GBs) to help stimulate the economy for higher growth under the guise of 'capital deepening', 'sensitive' sectors (for example, real estate/construction). It is worrying that some of the recent initiatives by the principal owner, like the quick-disbursing Mudra credit scheme, have been more akin to transfers.

The *government* is responsible for ensuring adequate capital for banks that are under its ambit on a durable/sustainable basis. The dominant owner pre-2014 didn't question risk controls in GBs even as it received significant dividends. A number of GBs did not have senior management in place, and governance suffered. This is a perennial shortcoming on account of bureaucratic inertia and political meddling. Ditto for the GBs' board of directors; it is common knowledge that this has traditionally been a placeholder for sinecure to political supporters. Key committees of the board, like the audit committee, have suffered from both inadequate membership, as seats go unfilled, as well as paucity of talent/domain knowledge to carry out fiduciary responsibilities to the level that is required and expected.

---

2 'Asset Quality of Indian Banks: Way Forward', Speech by N.S. Vishwanathan, delivered at National Conference of ASSOCHAM on Risk Management: Key to Asset Quality, New Delhi, August 2016.

The *regulator* fell short on several counts in the period leading up to 2014. It failed to challenge assumptions through, for example, more rigorous stress-test scenarios at bank level, as well as sensitivity analysis on (demand) assumptions, and sector (policy) risks. The scale of exposure – or risk build-up – was not appreciated enough and contested by the regulator to effectively slow down or tighten the lending norms, say, by increasing sector risk weights to ensure protection by increasing capital requirements.[3] India's credit practices have been informed, inter alia, by a confidence that income recognition and associated prudential parameters had scope for exceptions built in; lenders, led by the government, and large borrowers felt that the requisite leaning could lead to dilution. Implicitly, on balance, discretion is the default rather than the rule. An extenuating reality is that the regulator in our system does its work by constantly looking over its shoulder (Chapter 11). High professional integrity

---

3 In December 2010, the regulator did intervene on macro-prudential grounds in the context of an overheating housing sector. Banks were advised that the Loan to Value (LTV) ratio in respect of housing loans should not exceed 80 per cent. However, for small value housing loans, i.e., housing loans up to ₹2 million, the LTV ratio was capped at 90 per cent. The risk weight for residential housing loans of ₹7.5 million and above, irrespective of the LTV ratio, was pegged at 125 per cent. The standard asset provisioning on the outstanding amount of housing loans at teaser rates was increased from 0.4 per cent to 2 per cent. The provisioning on these assets was to revert to 0.4 per cent after one year from the date on which the rates are reset at higher rates if the accounts remain 'standard'. These steps were aimed at preventing excessive leveraging in housing loans' portfolio. (https://www.rbi.org.in/Scripts/NotificationUser.aspx?Id=6161&Mode=0)

notwithstanding, the RBI's reputation has been that of a soft regulator – deterrence has been undermined. In 2009/10, the RBI relaxed asset classification guidelines, which effectively allowed (large) borrowers to get more funding (ever greening) until as late as 2015, and for some categories even beyond; it is a 'win-win', viz., one stakeholder avoids default and the other can show low NPAs. Exposure norms as percentage of banks' capital funds were granted latitude; for instance, in February 2010, the RBI raised the exposure limit from 15 per cent to 20 per cent of capital funds for NBFCs that lent to infrastructure projects – by definition a high-risk sector.[4][5]

---

4 In January 2014, the risk weight and provisioning requirement on banks' exposures to entities having excessive unhedged forex exposure positions were increased, which was prudent.

5 From speech by N. S. Vishwanathan, 'Issues in Infrastructure Financing in India', 6th National Summit organized by ASSOCHAM on 'Infrastructure Finance - Building a New India', Mumbai, November 2016:

> The flow of bank finance to infrastructure sector has clocked high growth rates. The outstanding bank credit to the infrastructure sector, which stood at ₹95 billion in March 2001, increased to ₹9.85 trillion in March 2016, a compound annual growth rate of 39.31 percent over the last 15 years. This of course covers the period of excessive exuberance when it was fashionable to lend for road projects, power and the like, without the requisite due-diligence.

Given the well-known risks in the sector, the regulator could have resisted some of these demands.[6] The regulator, prior to 2014, not only neglected to take away the 'punch bowl' from the credit-binge 'party' – thereby missing an opportunity to signal that it is cognizant of a potential risk to sector stability – but may have contributed to spiking the 'punch bowl' by reinforcing forbearance through perpetuating practices like designating NPAs as standard restructured assets, a non sequitur.

The *supervisor's* role is to ensure that stringent risk-management processes and requirements are adhered to. There was a failure to acknowledge and rectify GBs' inability to identify poor performing assets; and restructure and react quickly to improve recovery or cut losses (by way of illustration, iron and steel companies, airlines, generators, real estate, etc.). The regulator's inspection reports rarely cautioned banks to the extent required about the high credit growth, which was running well ahead of real growth.

The *banks* themselves applied little risk analysis in sifting good from bad assets; they kept lending without much (or the requisite) due diligence, scepticism, concern for exposure concentration, high leverage and, overall, dynamic assessment over the cycle

---

6 It was in October 2016 that the RBI decisively brought large exposure norms to some semblance of sanity under the Large Exposure Framework, effective from 1 April 2019 (the time for transition was necessary). The single group exposure limit was brought down to 25 per cent from the erstwhile 40 per cent (plus add-'ons' up to 15 per cent), and the denominator was changed to eligible capital base (Tier 1) from total capital funds (Tier 1 plus Tier 2). Exposure to single NBFC was also brought down to 15 per cent of eligible capital.

(in other words, closed loop control was abjured). Inadequate risk management in banks didn't allow them to identify poor performing assets, and they may also have been in denial that there was a severe problem of poor quality assets (a build-up possibly as early as 2011 onwards). Instead, they seemed to have continued with extending further credit to poorly performing loan cases; this was done without commensurate enhancement of collateral;[7] borrowers seem to have proffered their name/personal net worth in the form of personal guarantees as substitute. Furthermore, some large borrowers, allegedly, may have taken equity out of the business (if investigations under way are anything to go by) or, at any rate, they did not inject more equity nor, it would seem, did the banks demand this as a precursor to further extension of credit. In other words, the scale, nature and complexity of these exposures were allowed to balloon out of hand.

The banks were too big to fail because the individual entities that they had lent to were deemed as too big to close down or change ownership. On an average, board-level firewalls did not fulfil remit adequately. Assets 'tucked away' by banks under the cloak provided by the Corporate Debt Restructuring cell were seriously impaired; these loans should have been evaluated for what they were – those meriting advance capital provisioning against likely recognition as NPAs in due course.

---

[7] For example, even when an airline was grounded, loans were being extended, presumably on account of 'name', which is a poor collateral (evidence: *on average* private sector banks/foreign banks are less exposed, and appear to have applied better risk management to manage their exposure).

GBs have argued incessantly over the decades – with mind-space capture of authorities and others – that an important reason for not calling out problem accounts in a timely manner as non-performing, hence legitimizing ever-greening, is that the government's vigilance agencies (the 3Cs, viz., the Central Bureau of Investigation [CBI], the Comptroller and Auditor General [CAG] and the Central Vigilance Commission [CVC]) would raise questions/initiate investigations and invite a form of retribution regarding why and how were these loans made. While the explanation may have merit, it is also puzzling at two levels: (i) GBs aren't shy of designating personal loans and advances to small borrowers as NPAs, and liquidating their security without fuss; and (ii) shouldn't GBs be more concerned about queries from the 3Cs when the loan size to struggling corporates is actually getting larger at a time when the latter's debt-servicing capability is obviously declining? How can more financing for essentially a restructured account be considered less serious than flagging an account as an NPA early in the life cycle of a loan? It would seem that the fear of the 3Cs is either a red herring or, at the least, an exaggeration behind which bankers take shelter to not do the right thing – that of protecting depositors' interest.

What about the *fourth and fifth stakeholders*? Not much to say here except for the deafening silence of otherwise voluble business associations on the subject of defaulting borrowers. There have hardly been any notable declarations supporting rules-based resolution and liquidation, or urging members to honour debt-servicing obligations. The dereliction is baffling, as the top leadership of business associations comprise bankers, and the carry cost of NPAs is driving up the margin on loans for *all* borrowers.

The financial media in the country routinely bestows banking awards on banks that have been fined, sometimes more than once, by sector regulators for transgressions. One would think that the rules for qualification would include, at a minimum, a transparent criterion that any bank that has been penalized by a regulator – since this has to be disclosed to the stock market, it makes for easy and costless verification – say, in the twelve months prior to the date of announcement of award, will not be considered. Further, there are instances of jury members affiliated to an institution that has been fined by a financial regulator. A reputation for abiding by regulations should matter. Is sponsorship of annual awards and banking conclaves worth the implicit condoning of wrongful actions?

As an example, consider the following. In July 2019, the regulator imposed fines on eleven banks for a wrongdoing. A few months later, in September 2019, one government bank in that list received an award from a financial publication. In October 2019, a private bank that had been punished in July won an award from another financial publication. One can go on, as there are other such instances.

In conclusion, all stakeholders were too slow and too late, and also possibly too naïve or in denial up to 2013/14. The RBI only started collating large exposure data in June 2014.[8] It is reasonable to conclude that stakeholders have been in reactive mode.

---

8 The RBI established the Central Repository of Information on Large Credits (CRILC) to collect, store and disseminate data on all borrowers' credit exposures, including Special Mention Accounts (SMA 0, 1 & 2) having aggregate fund-based and non-fund-based exposure of ₹50 million and above.

3
A TALE OF TWO SECTORS

THE BULK OF LARGE universal commercial banks in India are state-controlled for diverse (legacy) reasons, motivated by the polity's desire for government participation to steer policy and for social objectives. The government owns the majority share in numerous banks;[1] its holdings in GBs have further increased in the last ten years. Unusually for an annual fiscal statement, the Union budget ritually announces 'credit budgets' on behalf of banks. There are other 'quasi fiscal' drivers, with the list getting longer over time: the Mudra scheme for MSMEs in 2015; a 59-minute loan approval programme launched in late

---

1 In 2017 there were twenty-seven GBs. From April 2020 onwards, after some mergers, the number came down to twelve.

2018; and the Jan Dhan Yojana that was launched in mission mode with GBs as the primary instrument for universal bank account coverage. To counter the economic slowdown, in October 2019 banks, with due exhortation from the principal owner, undertook loan 'fairs' in rural areas to increase personal loans. Further, GBs provide employment to about 0.85 million employees, in aggregate, amongst the highest after the Indian Railways in civilian employment. It is sometimes posited, not wholly unfairly, that GBs predominantly deliver value on a sustained basis only to its large number of employees. The periodic sector-wide salary adjustment exercise for GBs has little to do with profitability and productivity; there is no material disparity in remuneration between GBs that make profits and those that don't.

A longstanding narrative that GBs are fundamentally safer than private banks (PBs) may be wearing thin. To illustrate, between March 2018 and March 2019, a period when there have been intermittent questions on banking sector stability, PBs have added more to their deposits as compared to GBs.[2] Of course, it remains to be seen how long the change will persist. There are two possible explanations for the evolution. One, the perception that deposits in GBs are underwritten by the sovereign, meaning that GBs are safer than PBs for the Indian *aam aadmi* depositors, may no longer hold as strongly as in the past; in other words, the social contract that is officially parlayed is not credible; news of

---

2 ₹4.8 trillion versus ₹2.3 trillion is the estimate after netting out the deposits of IDBI Bank upon its reclassification as a private bank.

bailouts and persistent losses are ubiquitous, and many people now connect the dots. Two, deposits are as safe, or unsafe, in PBs as they are in GBs, hence the depositor makes her choice mostly on service quality.

The contrast in performance between GBs and PBs is testimony to how government ownership undermines the baseline or normal financial discipline that is taken for granted in a broadly market-oriented economy. Chart 3.1 places India's banking sector alongside that of other major economies with respect to two variables: return on equity (RoE) and return on assets (RoA). For the financial year ending March 2019, both numbers are negative for the banking sector as a whole (IMF Financial Soundness Indicators and RBI's December 2019 Financial Stability Report [FSR]).

In contrast, if we bifurcate the sector between PBs and GBs, we find that for PBs, RoA and RoE are strongly positive. From the first lens metric of total financial returns, India's banking sector has outperformed the broader equity market (see Chart 3.2). However, GBs (bottom curve) have considerably underperformed as compared to both PBs (top curve) and the overall equity market (third curve).

Foreign portfolio investors have invested far more in PBs than compared to their shareholding in GBs (see Chart 3.3).

At the centre of the divergent financial outcomes of GBs with respect to PBs is the stock of NPAs on the respective balance sheets of the former compared to the latter (see Chart 3.4). Net NPAs of PBs are less than a third of GBs even after large infusion of capital into the latter by the government. Reinforcing the

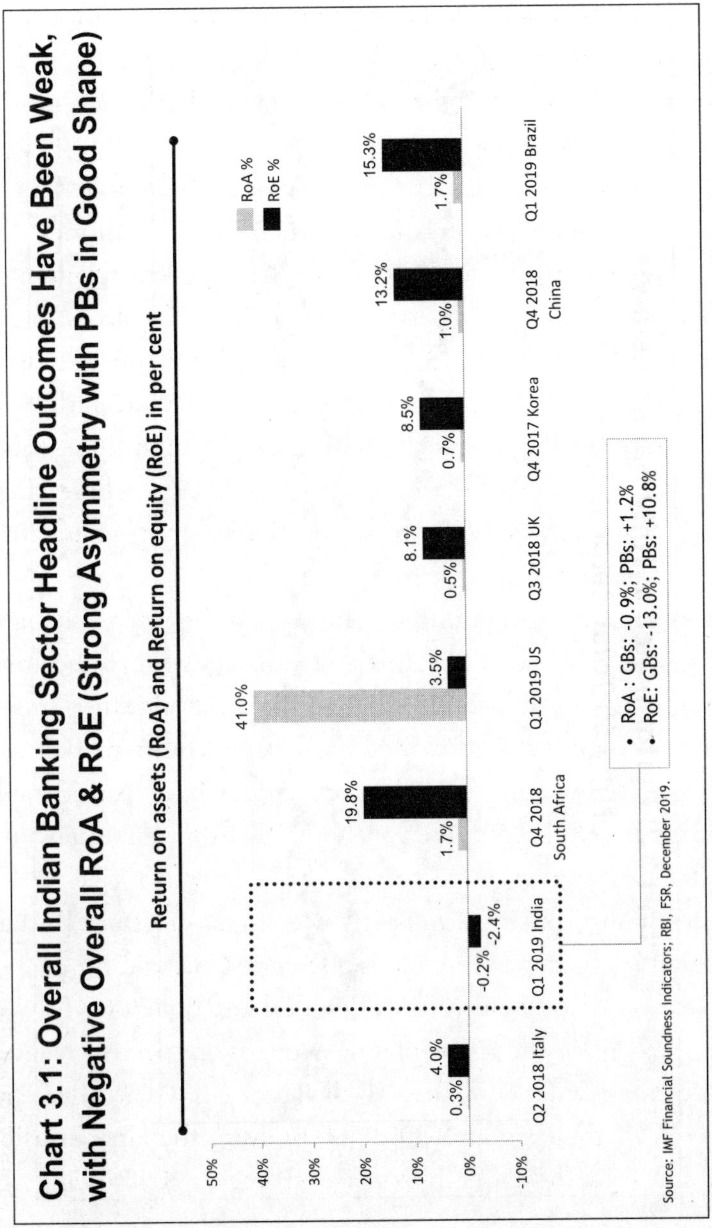

A Tale of Two Sectors

Chart 3.1: Overall Indian Banking Sector Headline Outcomes Have Been Weak, with Negative Overall RoA & RoE (Strong Asymmetry with PBs in Good Shape)

Return on assets (RoA) and Return on equity (RoE) in per cent

Country/Period	RoA %	RoE %
Q2 2018 Italy	0.3%	4.0%
Q1 2019 India	-0.2%	-2.4%
Q4 2018 South Africa	1.7%	19.8%
Q1 2019 US	3.5%	41.0%
Q3 2018 UK	0.5%	8.1%
Q4 2017 Korea	0.7%	8.5%
Q4 2018 China	1.0%	13.2%
Q1 2019 Brazil	1.7%	15.3%

- RoA : GBs: -0.9%; PBs: +1.2%
- RoE: GBs: -13.0%; PBs: +10.8%

Source: IMF Financial Soundness Indicators; RBI, FSR, December 2019.

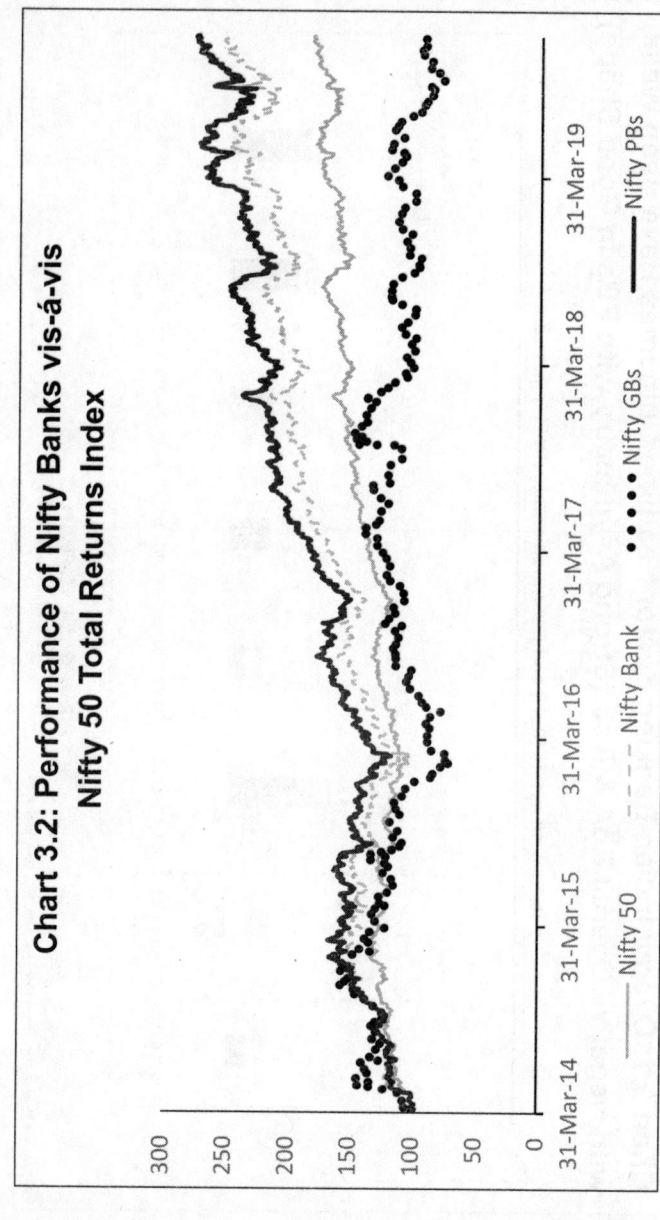

Chart 3.2: Performance of Nifty Banks vis-á-vis Nifty 50 Total Returns Index

Source: Stock market data.

A Tale of Two Sectors

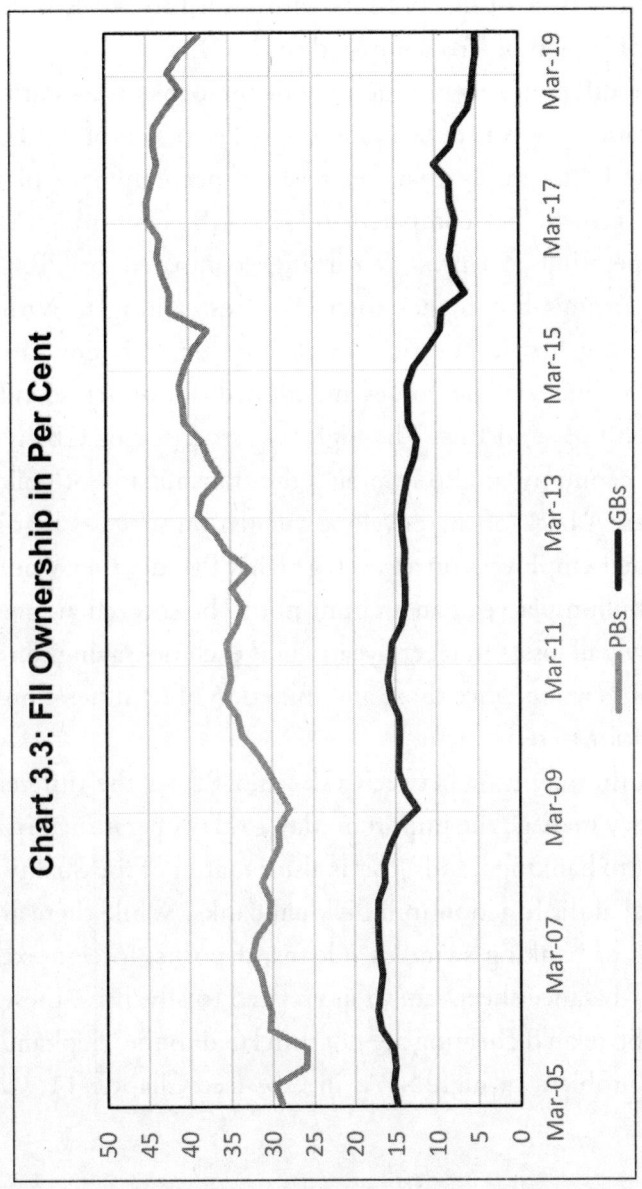

Source: Compiled from stock market data.

contrast between GBs and PBs with regard to NPAs is the high levels of capital of PBs compared to the GBs.

The difference in productivity of the banks is as stark as the NPA ratio. Revenue per employee and cost per employee between GBs and PBs imply that net revenue per employee of PBs is 50 per cent higher compared to GBs. GBs have a high ratio of non-operating expenses to earnings compared to PBs (lower opex/earnings but higher total expenses/earnings). With these contrasting first-level efficiency parameters, it is not surprising that the financial outcomes mentioned above are so different between GBs and PBs. The high cost structure of GBs is borne by the economy; it also impinges the transmission of policy rate changes. A back-of-the-envelope calculation suggests that if GBs paid their employees on an average what PBs do, they would save ₹380 billion per year, an amount not to be sneezed at, given the large overall losses in recent years. This excludes savings on future pension payouts since those are a function of remuneration in the years prior to retirement.

Another contrast between GBs and PBs is the difference in how they manage the important day-to-day operational risk with respect to banking frauds; this is also a matter of the quality of the internal audit function in individual banks. While there are four sources of banking swindles – loans, deposits, foreign exchange and off-balance sheet – most are related to advances; these levels of credit-related cheating are not unrelated to the 'elephant in the room' problem of high NPAs in GBs (see Chapter 11, Chapter

A Tale of Two Sectors

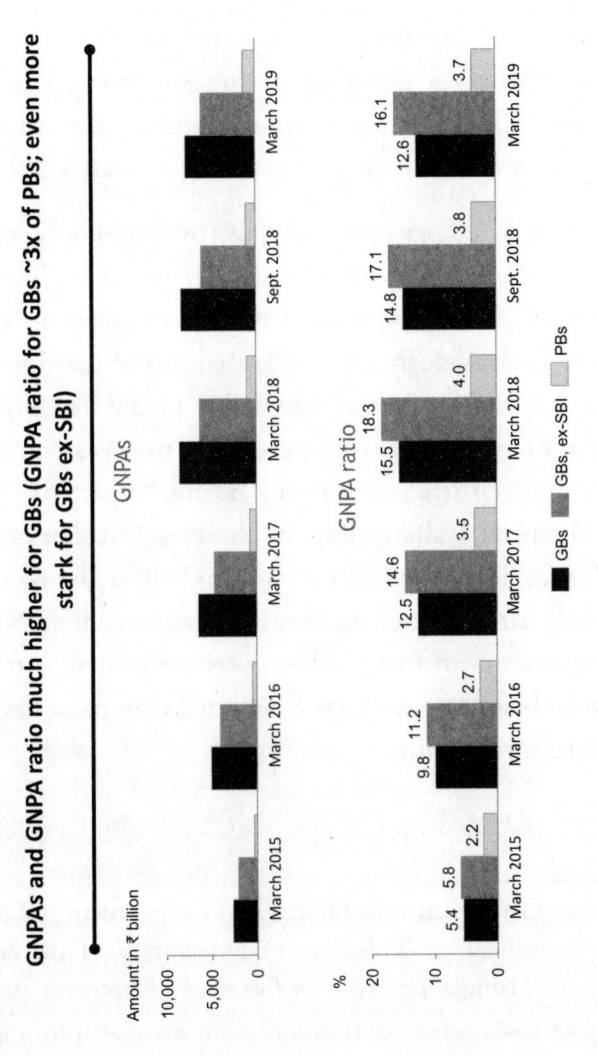

Chart 3.4: The NPA Issue Has Largely Been Driven by GBs

GNPAs and GNPA ratio much higher for GBs (GNPA ratio for GBs ~3x of PBs; even more stark for GBs ex-SBI)

Source: Statistical tables relating to banks in India; RBI, FSR; RBI, Annual Reports.

13 and Report of the Expert Committee on NPAs and Frauds [2018]).[3]

'...[T]here is the third kind of problem with public sector bank lending – pervasive corruption from branches to regional offices in sanctioning and writing off a vast number of smaller loans.' – *Business Standard*, 4 March 2019[4]

As many as 90 per cent of frauds (by value) occurred in GBs, while the share of PBs is less than 8 per cent. The reported quantum of frauds has quadrupled in the five years since 2013/14; it is very likely that frauds committed in the past have come to light in the last few years in part due to the pressure from the regulator for banks to be transparent and the insistence, including enforcement, of strict accounting norms.[5] The RBI's December 2019 Financial Stability Report observes that cases of fraud of over ₹10 billion increased by a multiple over the previous year. In January 2020, one of the twelve largest corporate NPAs in the banking system, of ₹140 billion, was designated as fraud, three years after being referred to the National Company Law Tribunal (NCLT) for resolution.

---

3   What a GB executive said in late 2019 is instructive: 'Lenders were not policemen' or 'Enforcement Directorate'; 'How do you deal with shell companies?' (*Indian Express*, 17 December 2019, p. 16).

4   https://www.business-standard.com/article/opinion/psbs-get-money-while-rbi-mof-get-away-again-119030400017_1.html

5   The vast majority of frauds are high value – ₹500 million or more.

B: CLEANSING THE AUGEAN STABLES

4

THE FIRST 4RS: RECOGNIZE THE REALITY, RECORD, REPORT, RECOVERY[1]

Take Head out of the Sand

THE SIZE AND NATURE of the NPA problem necessitated commensurate measures to signal the intent and commitment of the government and the RBI. The challenge began to be addressed squarely in a coherent manner in mid-

---

1 In various sections of Chapters 4, 5, 6, 8 and 16, text from the following speeches and presentations has been used: 'Resolution of Stressed Assets – Towards the Endgame', Inaugural Session of the

2014, with a regulatory, legal and institutional thrust, the first phase of which was completed in 2016.

The establishment of the Central Repository of Information on Large Credits (CRILC) by the Reserve Bank in May 2014 filled a critical breach in addressing information asymmetry regarding NPAs at the system level by facilitating collection of data on credit exposures across the banking system.[2] It helped, in a structured manner, focus on multiple information gaps: between banks and the regulator, amongst banks, and concerning the banking regulator and the government courtesy the Financial Stability and Development Council (FSDC), the systemic overseer chaired by the finance minister. Having the aggregate view of borrower-wise and bank-wise exposures provided the requisite first-level information dashboard for supervisors and

---

National Conference on Insolvency and Bankruptcy: Changing Paradigm, Mumbai, August 2017; 'Managing Post-Crisis Banking and Financial Sector Challenges: Indian Experience', Presentation at the 2017 Governors' Symposium of the Association of African Central Banks, Pretoria, August 2017; 'Banking Regulatory Powers Should Be Ownership-Neutral', Inaugural Lecture at the Centre for Law & Economics, Centre for Banking & Financial Laws, Gujarat National Law University, Gandhinagar, March 2018.

2 The RBI set up CRILC to collect, store and disseminate data on all borrowers' credit exposures including Special Mention Accounts (SMA 0, 1 & 2) with aggregate fund-based and non-fund-based exposure of ₹50 million and above. Credit information to CRILC is submitted by all scheduled commercial banks (excluding regional rural banks). There is a similar CRILC system for NBFCs with reporting of credit information by the top seventy NBFCs.

policymakers, as well as lenders, to track the incipient stress in a particular account in a timely manner. It assisted the macro-prudential observer, the FSDC, in appreciating the full, complex, interconnected scale of the malaise in credit markets. Without CRILC it would have been, if not virtually impossible, time-consuming to confidently assess the exposure to, and quality of, large loans. In CRILC's absence, the regulator was steering by looking at the rearview mirror. Instead of getting a snapshot, which is what supervisory reports do, CRILC provided dynamic real-time – or at any rate with a short lag – information. And the purported asymmetry of information between banks stopped the *gaming* by wily borrowers.[3] It is noteworthy that there was foot-dragging initially by some banks to effectively implement the information technology protocol at their end for CRILC to function in a timely and effective manner. Was it the case that at least some banks were deliberately delaying the sharing of information with the regulator?

Asset Quality Review of Banks Undertaken by the RBI: A Case of Sifting through the Debris

The Asset Quality Review (AQR) exercise was initiated in the second half of 2015 because banks were hiding problem assets. The clean-up started with a candid assessment of the sloth hiding

---

[3] Gaming was cited by bankers as an excuse for unknowingly ever-greening loans of large borrowers. If true, borrowers were breaking loan covenants that always require sharing information with every lender on all existing loans as a pre-condition.

in the sector's balance sheet. Not surprisingly, large delinquent accounts at a number of banks had to be revised upwards. There was a threefold increase in *disclosed* NPAs for GBs from the levels of 2013/14. For the PBs, there was a doubling in reported NPAs. PBs had to raise capital from markets to shore up capital ratios and initiate a buffer for higher provisioning; all barring one have done this relatively easily.[4]

Around one-sixth of GBs' gross advances were found, at first pass, to be stressed (non-performing, restructured or written-off), and a greater part of these were bad debts. For some banks, the share of assets under stress approached or exceeded 20 per cent. The estimate of stressed assets had doubled from 2013 in terms of what had been recognized by banks and acknowledged by the RBI (see Acharya [2017]).[5] While the (revised) stressed assets of PBs also witnessed a very large jump, their ratio of stressed assets to gross advances was appreciably lower and their levels of regulatory capital were much larger.

In summary, the AQR was a form of catch-up to reality. In tandem, a series of measures were put in place by the regulator to provide a path for coordinated revival of problem loans and recovery of value.

---

4 The exception being the fourth largest private bank, although it did manage to raise fresh equity capital in March 2017 and August 2019.

5 'Some Ways to Decisively Resolve Bank Stressed Assets', Speech by Viral Acharya delivered at the Indian Banks' Association Banking Technology Conference, Mumbai, February 2017.

The First 4Rs

The Framework for Revitalising Distressed Assets in the Economy in January 2014 was 'developed [by] outlining a corrective action plan that will incentivise early identification of problem accounts, timely restructuring of accounts which are considered to be viable, and taking prompt steps by lenders for recovery or sale of unviable accounts'.[6] It sought to address coordination problems in large consortium accounts and, therefore, envisaged the constitution of the Joint Lenders' Forum (JLF).

Further, since the Insolvency and Bankruptcy Code was then still work in progress, additional tools to assist with the recovery of problem assets were introduced as a stopgap in the absence of a comprehensive mechanism. A regulatory structure was put in place for greater transparency in sale of stressed assets by banks with a view to ensure that the transaction was at market-determined prices. The tools, the so-called 'alphabet soup' (listed below), were primarily aimed at structuring of credit facilities, smoothening change of ownership and to aid the restructuring of loans; a couple of these facilitated little more than 'extend and pretend', that is, only kicked the can down the road.

- The Strategic Debt Restructuring (SDR) Mechanism was introduced in February 2014 (and revised in June 2015).
- The 5:25 scheme was introduced in July 2014 and its scope was extended in December 2014.
- The Scheme for Sustainable Structuring of Stressed Assets (S4A) was notified in June 2016.

---

6 https://rbidocs.rbi.org.in/rdocs/content/pdfs/NPA300114RFF.pdf

The guidelines provided for an Overseeing Committee (OC), an advisory body with persons of eminence as members, to be constituted by the Indian Banks' Association (IBA) in consultation with the RBI. The JLF could refer resolution plans and one-time settlement proposals worth more than ₹5 billion to the OC. By vetting the processes followed for reasonableness and adherence to the provisions of the guidelines, the OC was to be a source of comfort to bankers, who had been worried about overzealous scrutiny from investigative agencies.

The pathways mentioned above provided generous timelines but with precious little to show. For instance, under the SDR option, available since early 2014, there were hardly any notable successful takeovers by lenders of large assets through conversion of debt into a majority equity stake, even as late as 2017.

One of the key problems was the dissenting creditor exception that held up the restructuring process in many cases. In other words, what economists call the inherent agency and incentive failures due to pivotal voting constrained the JLFs from achieving the very objective they were constituted for.

5

THE 5TH R: RESOLUTION

SOME STAKEHOLDERS AND COMMENTATORS had proposed that we should 'house' stressed assets above a certain ticket size in a special purpose vehicle, to sanitize the banking sector's balance sheet in one fell swoop, thereby freeing banks to make a new start for lending. There was a fair bit of discussion between the government and the RBI in 2015 and 2016 on the subject of 'bad bank'.[1] At the highest levels of policymaking the idea was

---

1 A note was prepared in October 2015 to make a case for a Special Purpose Power Assets Bank (SPPAB) entitled: 'Is it time for an eclectic/hybrid approach for rehabilitating the banking balance sheet? Some considerations for creating a "bad bank".'

not liked, mainly because borrowers and lenders would be off the hook, and it was in the nature of 'mother of all moral hazard' – an undesirable backdrop for the next lending cycle. Both the government and the RBI were convinced that incentives had to be preserved. It was felt that the decentralized marketplace for distressed assets, which the Insolvency and Bankruptcy Code was designed to encourage and support, would impart greater accountability on stakeholders. A blanket bailout of the type that is entailed in the 'bad bank' structure would have been difficult to justify, hence it was possibly also politically unpalatable.

Legal Framework for Resolution

In May 2016, the Insolvency and Bankruptcy Code (IBC) was enacted as a watershed towards strengthening India's financial architecture; it was overdue and, quite correctly, it is universally acknowledged as a landmark reform. It is a modern code which empowers creditors to take the necessary action upon failure to pay. Default, even by a day, of at least ₹100,000, allows a creditor, financial or operational, to file a reference in the National Company Law Tribunal (NCLT).[2] Prior to the IBC, India had multiple laws that governed various facets of a corporate rescue and/or insolvency, without having an up-to-date comprehensive legal structure that envisages a holistic process applicable to troubled or defaulting companies. The IBC provides for a single-window, time-bound route for resolution of an asset with an explicit emphasis on promotion of entrepreneurship (not

---

2   In March 2020 the floor was raised to ₹10 million.

preservation of entrenched defaulter elite), maximization of value of assets, and balancing the interests of stakeholders. The extant Securitization and Reconstruction of Financial Assets and Enforcement of Security Interest Act, 2002 (SARFAESI), and Recovery of Debts Due to Banks and Financial Institutions Act, 1993 (RDDBFI; DRT for short), had become toothless – on average, recovery was barely a quarter and that too after four years of litigation.

The most significant cost to a sponsor being compelled under the IBC may be the possibility of losing the firm to potential bidders. This should incentivize firms to avoid defaults and not over-borrow; it reinforces, ex ante, the incentive to borrow sensibly and dutifully service debt.

For a creditor, an asset, in most cases, is more valuable when it is a going concern and generating cash flow, as compared to an asset under liquidation. The IBC puts a time limit of 180 days (extendable by a further ninety days) within which creditors have to agree to a resolution plan, failing which the adjudicating authority under the law will pass a liquidation order on the insolvent company. Those lenders interested in recovery of money had been empowered to take recourse to a clear process. So the threat of liquidation, which could potentially result in larger losses for creditors, should be sufficient incentive for them to coordinate during the resolution period and quickly arrive at a decision.

Belated response did not work in the area of resolution

The envisaged self-correction did not transpire. The IBC was in place for salvaging value in loan assets that had failed but banks were not forthcoming with the requisite initiative in respect of large stressed accounts. 'Living-dead' borrowers were still dominant in bank balance sheets in 2017. 'Only a bank that fears losing its deposit base or incurring the wrath of its shareholders is likely to recognize losses in a timely manner. In many of our banks, such market discipline is simply not present at the moment' (Acharya [2017]).[3] Inaction by banks against large defaulters undermined the credibility of a major legal and institutional reform designed to improve the allocative efficiency of the economy. The sluggishness of banks was eroding assets worth, at book value, around ₹10 trillion. In 2016, the share of large accounts in total advances was roughly 55 per cent, and their share in total NPAs was about 85 per cent.

Much of the inertia was due to the typical and severe agency and *aggravated* moral hazard problems of not resolving NPAs when the banking sector was majorly government owned. The *unconstrained discretion*, of whether to invoke the IBC or not, rather than a *binding rule* for the large defaults had led to *corner* outcomes – that is, being observed in the breach or inaction. At the same time, since the AQR, as the skeletons came tumbling out, a question mark over banking sector stability periodically reared its head (see Chart 5.1).

---

3 Op. cit.

The 5th R: Resolution

Chart 5.1: ...Even as There Has Been Intermittent Concern Over Sector Health

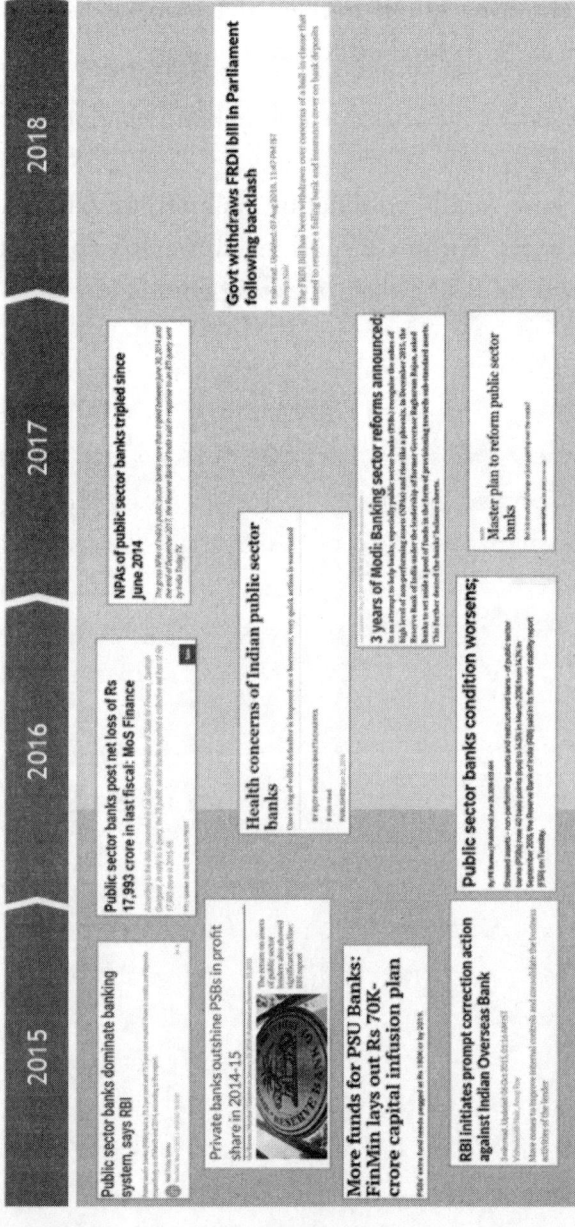

The above backdrop implied that two key shortcomings in the framework had to be addressed quickly:

- Absence of a hard-coded, time-bound period for resolution; and
- Agency and coordination failures at banks and Joint Lenders' Forums in pushing through viable restructuring plans or, failing that, initiating liquidation.

6

THE 6TH R: REINFORCED RESOLUTION – CUTTING THE GORDIAN KNOT

MARKET FAILURE, DESCRIBED EARLIER, necessitated, in 2017, further steps by the government and the Reserve Bank to confront the promoter–bank relationship by strengthening the legal and regulatory scaffolding. The sense of urgency imbued in the action by the two stakeholders in tandem was reflective of the goal of not allowing things to drag any further. The measures were in the nature of *constrained discretion*. Because empowered lenders were not acting to manage incipient risks and recover assets, the regulator had to be proactive.

On the resolution side, steps were aimed at facilitating a time-bound, but not necessarily hurried, resolution of stressed assets. The government took an unprecedented initiative by modifying a key legislation in 2017. The Banking Regulation (BR) (Amendment) Act, 2017, in Sections 35 AA and 35 AB, empowers the RBI to issue directions to banking companies to initiate an insolvency resolution process in respect of a default, under the provisions of the IBC. It enabled the Reserve Bank to issue directions 'with respect to stressed assets and specify one or more authorities or committees with such members as the Bank may appoint or approve for appointment to advise banking companies on resolution of stressed assets'.[1]

To help streamline decision making amongst lenders, the norms for consent required for approval of a proposal was changed to 60 per cent by value instead of 75 per cent, as earlier. Banks that were in the minority on the proposal approved by the JLF were required to either exit by complying with the substitution rules within the stipulated time or adhere to the decision of the JLF; cram-downs were now feasible. The participating banks were mandated to implement the decision of the JLF without any additional conditionality. Also, the boards of directors of respective banks were advised to empower executives to implement JLF decisions without further reference to them. It was felt that these instructions from the regulator, aimed at reducing the coordination problems among lenders while trying

---

[1] https://www.rbi.org.in/SCRIPTS/BS_PressReleaseDisplay.aspx?prid=40518

to resolve stressed assets outside the purview of the IBC, would induce speedier decisions amongst the lenders.

During the annual financial inspection of individual banks, divergences between the NPAs and provisions declared by the banks and those assessed by inspectors came to light; this has harmful implications on the timely recognition of actual risk, the trustworthiness and transparency of books of accounts, internal compliance rules and management effectiveness. Accordingly, in order to address infirmities, disclosure requirements have now been put in place – banks have to divulge, in their account filing, the details of such divergences that exceed the specified thresholds.

The regulator took further proactive steps. On systemic risk management, the RBI, in April 2017, advised banks to 'put in place a board–approved policy for making provisions for standard assets at rates higher than the regulatory minimum, based on evaluation of risk and stress in various sectors'. The board policy had to be reviewed regularly keeping in mind the dynamic nature of sector-specific strains.[2] The interest coverage ratio for the telecom sector was less than one at the time; hence, it directed the boards of banks to review exposures to the sector within three months. The purpose was to goad banks subject their exposures to the sector into closer monitoring and build resilience in their balance sheets.

In the wake of some high-profile frauds and governance failures that came to light with the Punjab National Bank saga and the use of the SWIFT system, internal discussions commenced

---

2 https://rbidocs.rbi.org.in/rdocs/notification/PDFs/NT2820702162075B94A7AAC68A019D4329D2A.PDF.

within the RBI to carve out a specialized supervisory cadre to meet the challenges of a financial system getting even more complex and technology driven. Such developments, inter alia, called for dedicated expertise at the regulator level as well. Hence, after thorough brainstorming across departments, the idea was presented to members of the Central Board in April 2018. On getting its concurrence, focused effort was entrusted to a special team within the RBI culminating in a formal approval by the board in May 2019.

Overseeing Committee

In order to strengthen the role of the Overseeing Committee (OC), the Reserve Bank brought the OC under its backing with support from the IBA. This was necessary to reinforce the statute-backed authority of the OC to review the processes and provide requisite comfort to the lenders to agree to market-determined haircuts as part of restructuring. In June 2017, the OC was reconstituted with an expanded scope and membership. While it continued to oversee cases being restructured under the S4A, the reconstituted OC's expanded mandate was also to review resolution of all those cases where the banking sector's aggregate exposure to a single borrower exceeded ₹5 billion.

Evolving Regulatory Framework: Follow-up Action by the Reserve Bank

On the basis of the aforementioned legislation amendment, the Reserve Bank started work towards ascertaining a set of accounts to be referred for resolution under IBC, based on the recommendations of an Internal Advisory Committee (IAC) comprising members of the Bank's Central Board of Directors. The process adopted for identifying the entities was consistent with the object of making the speediest recovery of economic value. The classification criteria recommended by the IAC was based on 'an intelligible differentia comprising quantum, materiality, as well as age of the NPA' – effectively how long an account was (unsuccessfully) seasoning in one of the 'alphabet soup' schemes cited in Chapter 4.

It must be emphasized, however, that being referred for insolvency process under the IBC does not necessarily mean that the borrower company is being liquidated. It simply puts a timeline within which the various stakeholders have to come up with a feasible resolution plan, including sale as a going concern, to be approved by the Committee of Creditors constituted under the aegis of the NCLT; only if the effort fails would the company end up in liquidation.

Pointed End of the Spear: Outcome

For about two years, banks had not been able to do much about large restructured standard assets – an oxymoron, if ever there was one – despite the broad leeway granted by the regulator. In June and September 2017, the regulator, on the recommendation of the IAC, directed banks to file, for resolution in the NCLT, forty-one of the largest defaulting corporations – with an aggregate exposure of ₹5 trillion – that accounted for approximately 45 per cent of NPAs at the time.

Enforcement Action by the RBI

Weak credit discipline in banks, right from the appraisal to the sanction stage, has been one of the main bank-specific factors in the build-up of stressed assets. The risk-based supervisory process of the Reserve Bank keeps flagging risks in the balance sheet of banks, which are taken up with the management of these institutions for remedy; but firm and coherent steps on the specific violations/breaches has been a gap in implementation.[3] In order to aid effective enforcement action on the specific violations/breaches, a separate Enforcement Department was established by the RBI; it brought us in line with other Central banks. The mandate of the department comprises development and execution of a guideline-based decision ladder to deal with breaches of law, rules and directions. Effective deterrence enforced through such actions is expected to contribute towards strengthening the overall credit culture. Steps were initiated at the October 2016 meeting of the RBI Central Board, and the department started its work in April 2017.

---

3   It is possible that over the years a form of 'Stockholm syndrome' had clouded action. Supervision teams all too often tend to come up with mitigating explanations for not recommending apposite strictures and penalties commensurate with transgressions that have been brought to light.

7

THE 7TH R: RECAPITALIZATION AND THE FISCAL DIMENSION

IN SEPTEMBER 2017, A key component of the jigsaw fell into place after extensive consultations between the regulator and the finance ministry.

A two-year recapitalization plan for GBs was rolled out; it was a strong policy statement supportive of the continuing NPA clean-up while ensuring financial stability. The latter consideration was important as losses at GBs mounted up on account of continuing provision for bad assets. The proposed Financial Resolution and

Deposit Insurance (FRDI) legislation had to be withdrawn in 2017 due to doubts that were raised on banking sector stability on social media and elsewhere. The bail-in provision, which applied to a narrow set of depositors, was used as a handle by detractors to alarm the government.

Banking sector recapitalization can take several forms:

1. Direct cash infusion by government and public financial institutions.
2. Issuing budget-neutral recap bonds.
3. Raising capital (equity, sub-debt) from the market.
4. Divestment of equity holding in joint ventures, special purpose vehicles and asset management companies. Realization of capital gains on investments (as promoter) in these subsidiaries can be used to beef up capital reserves and make provisions.
5. Subscription by GBs and financial institutions to each other's Tier-II capital, through cross purchase of papers, similar to 'double gearing' (à la Japanese banks). Alternatively, non-voting preference shares may be issued. Apart from considerations of following up on directives from the government-owner of these intermediaries, this practice – popular in the first decade and a half of the millennium – was also a reflection of fears of poor market appetite for subscribing to Tier-I or Tier-II capital. Given the state of banks at that juncture, it was akin to rearranging the deck chairs on the *Titanic*.

The 7th R: Recapitalization and the Fiscal Dimension

The first two modes inevitably increase the government's stake in GBs. Except for the last two to three years, much of the recapitalization has been in the form of direct equity infusion from the budget. In 2017/18 and 2018/19, this was supplanted by issuing recap bonds that GBs subscribe to, and the money was used by the government to buy equity in the same banks. The immediate and recurring cash outgo for the government is the interest payment on the recap bonds (which also contributes to GBs' top line). Of course, the stock of government liabilities goes up by the quantum of recap bonds issued, as these will have to be redeemed at maturity. From a housekeeping perspective, recap via issuance of bonds is supposed to help towards nursing GBs to profitability and, in due course, dividends to the government will help the latter redeem them. At least, that is the theory.

- Around ₹1.9 trillion has been injected by the principal owner into GBs in 2017/18 and 2018/19.
- Life Insurance Corporation of India's investment of ₹216.2 billion into a GB in 2018 took the total capital support in the two fiscal years to ₹2.1 trillion.[1]
- In the first round (early 2018), even the largest GB required support.

And it (inevitably) goes on!

A further ₹700 billion has been infused by the government in 2019/20 with the entire quantum by way of recap bonds. This

---

1 This brought the estimated aggregate infusion 2010/11–2018/19 to ₹3.1 trillion.

amount is almost double of independent analysts' initial estimates in early 2019; much of the capital will be for bridging regulatory capital shortfall and provisioning for ageing impaired loans.

Innovative schemes in the smoke-and-mirrors genre have been hatched up. The government-owned LIC and State Bank of India (SBI) in 2019 have been directed by the finance ministry to pony up ₹150 billion towards a fund to provide financing to already over-leveraged problematic real-estate projects that are 'close to completion'. Moreover, even as the spillover onto banks of other intermediaries has been a concern for the latter's health, the government has agreed to underwrite 10 per cent of banks' purchase of up to one trillion rupees of NBFC debt. Surely, this does not de-risk matters! Separately, the government's general insurance companies are now also short of capital and in queue for recap. The long shadow of moral hazard only gets broader.

The success and credibility of the resolution efforts detailed above are also critically contingent on the strength of the official balance sheet to absorb the costs. It is clear that GBs will need to take haircuts on exposures under any resolution plan agreed within or outside the IBC. Higher provisioning requirements, on this count as well as other factors – for example, the economic slowdown – will affect the capital position of several banks. This may necessitate further recapitalization looking into the future. Capacity for more capital support by the principal owner is a function of the *fiscal space*. How much is available? One candidate metric is the difference between the extant general government debt/GDP ratio and targets that the government has picked (Chart 7.1).

The 7th R: Recapitalization and the Fiscal Dimension

Comparing the laudable medium-term general government debt targets laid out in the Fiscal Responsibility and Budget Management (FRBM) roadmap to the *present* level suggests that there is hardly any elbow room. Combined with the (implicit) comfort and support to depositors, a broader question of which liabilities of the government to include when evaluating public debt outstanding and (in)solvency naturally arises.[2]

For sure, the public sector includes Central, state and local governments; public enterprises (which are not included in the FRBM objectives); and the Central bank. Inclusion (or not) of government-owned commercial banks is a judgement call; the extent of 'arm's length' is, perhaps, the most important consideration (Buiter and Patel [2006])[3]. If it is not 100 per cent certain that the long arm of the sovereign extends to servicing some of the obligations of GBs, consolidation will overstate the true indebtedness. Alternatively, if, as seems to be increasingly the case, preservation of depositors' interests is interpreted as a social contract between the government and the public that (virtually?) guarantees all bank deposits in GBs, then these particular liabilities are not just a contingent financial responsibility of the Central government, they are actual obligations. However, general government securities and public sector debt (loans) held (advanced) by GBs will then have to be netted out for consistency. Back-of-the-envelope calculations for 2017/18

---

2 Legally, deposit insurance of up to ₹500,000 per depositor is provided.

3 Op. cit.

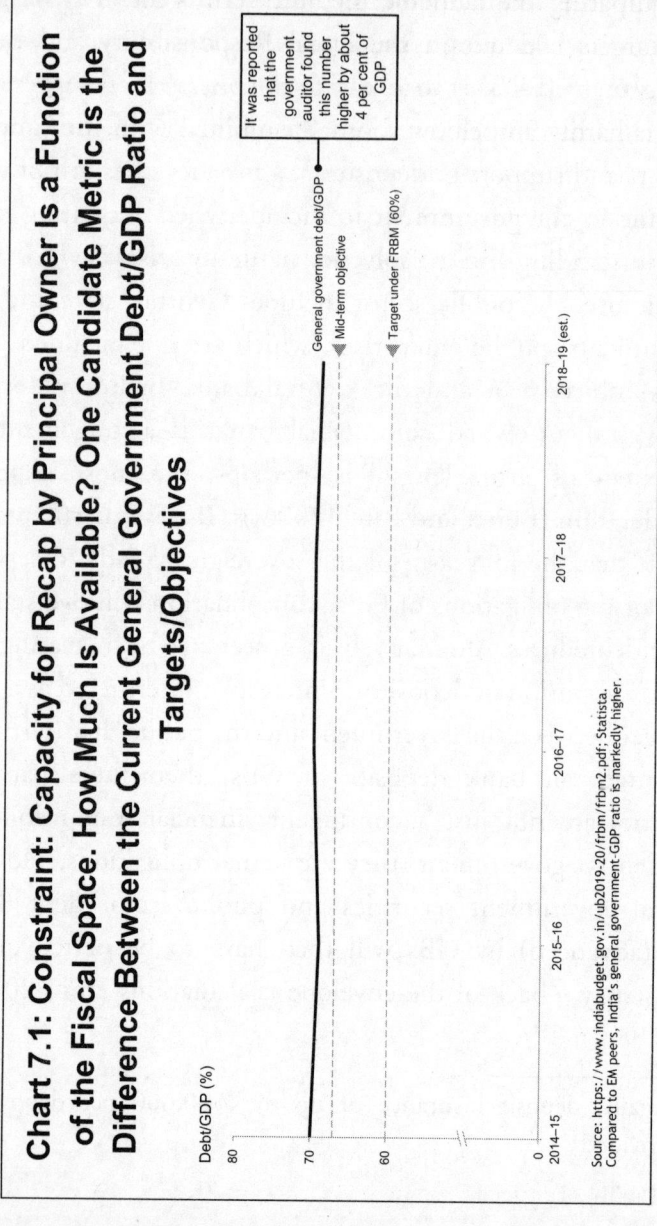

Chart 7.1: Constraint: Capacity for Recap by Principal Owner Is a Function of the Fiscal Space. How Much Is Available? One Candidate Metric is the Difference Between the Current General Government Debt/GDP Ratio and Targets/Objectives

Source: https://www.indiabudget.gov.in/ub2019-20/frbm/frbm2.pdf; Statista.
Compared to EM peers, India's general government-GDP ratio is markedly higher.

The 7th R: Recapitalization and the Fiscal Dimension

based on accepted methodology (Buiter and Patel [2012])[4] give the following estimates, as per cent of GDP, for official gross total debt (80 per cent), net total debt (64 per cent), and augmented net total debt (96 per cent).[5] As the length of the arm between banks and the sovereign shortens or even disappears, and if we continue to play fast and loose with banks, rating agencies and bond vigilantes will turn their gaze to the largest of the three debt ratios above.

---

4 'Fiscal Rules in India: Are They Effective?' in Chetan Ghate (ed.), *The Handbook of the Indian Economy*, Oxford University Press, Oxford and New York, 2012.

5 Comprehensive, aggregate local government debt numbers are not available; neither is the consolidated debt of state government-owned enterprises; to that extent, the estimates here may understate the level of official indebtedness.

8

THE 8TH R: RESET AND RING-FENCE TO CEMENT THE CHANGE

Fortifying the Transformation Ushered in 2017

THE 6TH R AND the 7th R provided opportunities for taking two further complementary steps in a calibrated manner. The regulator's 12 February 2018 regulations were introduced to prod banks towards timely recognition of problem assets and initiate restructuring, failing which NCLT-based resolution/insolvency had to be used.[1] The IBC/NCLT is, for defaulters,

---

1 https://rbidocs.rbi.org.in/rdocs/notification/PDFs/131DBRCEC9D8FEED1C467C9FC15C74D01745A7.PDF

The 8th R: Reset and Ring-Fence to Cement the Change

about as welcome as Kryptonite is for the comic-book hero Superman.

Within the compass of the BR Act Amendments, a decision process for the balance of large problematic exposures needed to be initiated after the forty-one large (mature) defaulting cases were referenced. The IAC, a sub-committee of the central board of the RBI, was of the view that: (i) in the absence of rules, the IAC would have become a *standing committee* for assessing which defaulters should be referenced to the NCLT for resolution; (ii) a case-by-case process would increase the likelihood of legal challenges as, quite correctly, the extant process may be perceived as ad hoc, consequently discriminatory, and hence unfair by the initial sets of references, with exposures of at least ₹30 billion, which were recommended to the banks; and (iii) putting in place a simple set of forward-looking regulations would enhance allocative efficiency as all stakeholders were now aware of the path with respect to defaults, legacy and the future.

The revised framework for resolution of stressed assets was a conduit for steering the initial steps of 2017 described above to their natural conclusion by laying down a *steady-state rule* that had close rationale and nexus with the underlying intention of the IBC and modifications in the BR Act. The approach was aimed at timely resolution of legacy stressed assets with greater predictability, to help realize maximum value for lenders by prioritizing the potential ongoing concern worth of the company's assets. It reset power between borrower and lender.

'I was in the banking industry for thirty-six years, but I don't remember a single circular being as powerful as the one issued on 12 February 2018...' – Former chairman and managing director of a GB[2]

'It is a very good circular, and no major dilution is needed. It set a clear-cut boundary line and gave full freedom to banks.' – CEO, Indian Banks' Association (IBA)[3]

'The streamlining of the NPA resolution process affords simplicity, timeliness and credibility, so is a long-term positive for the banking sector.' – press release by CRISIL Ratings[4]

The February 2018 circular removed uncertainty – it brought the sector regulator's rules in line with the letter and spirit of the IBC 2016, and a retune along three dimensions towards defining an endgame:[5]

8.A Various special schemes for resolution, which were introduced by the RBI in the pre-IBC context,

---

[2] 'How RBI's Feb 12 Circular Changed the Way Banks Dealt with Stressed Assets', *Economic Times*, 10 February 2019.

[3] 'What is RBI's February 12 circular all about?', *Business Standard*, 12 February 2019.

[4] Source: https://www.ndtv.com/topic/press-trust-of-india, Press Trust of India, 14 February 2019.

[5] See my lecture 'Banking Regulatory Powers should be Ownership Neutral', Inaugural Lecture at the Centre for Law & Economics, Centre for Banking & Financial Laws, Gujarat National Law University, Gandhinagar, March 2018; and the cogent article: Richa Roy, 'Deny Defaulters Their Paradise', *Economic Times*, 13 May 2019.

had made the resolution process driven by asset classification consideration of lenders. The decision to do away with the prolonged and ineffective – except for the defaulters – regulatory forbearance regarding asset classification on restructuring of loans and advances operative from April 2015 was a significant step from the perspective of aligning the regulatory norms with international best practices.

- The ploy of restructured standard assets, which had started about two decades back with circulars on Corporate Debt Restructuring 2001, 2002 and 2005, had to be buried once and for all.
- The assortment of schemes of recent vintage, introduced as interim instruments, to fill the void pending the legislated IBC could now be closed. It is noteworthy that the track record of these, even after a generous/inordinate period of time, for any resolution was, without exaggeration, poor. The forbearance that was embedded to make it easier to resolve assets became an end in itself; they essentially delayed formal acknowledgement that an account was an NPA.

8.B New prudential norms for banks regarding asset classification and provisioning. It removed discretion on what constitutes default, which, ipso facto, pushes lenders to initiate matters:

- Immediately on default, accounts had to be classified as Special Mention Accounts (SMA); and,

- As a natural consequence, the resolution process was to start within a day of default.

8.C Time-bound discretion followed by a rule:

It further required that if accounts of the defaulting large borrowers were not resolved within six months from the date on which their instalments fell due, then they had no choice but to refer these accounts for recovery/liquidation to the NCLT.

Asset viability considerations were paramount and these, any lender worth his/her salt would agree, require timely action. The revised framework allowed lenders absolute flexibility to put in place *any* credible resolution plan subject to meeting certain implementation conditions against the touchstone of apposite rating by independent agencies – these being necessary to alleviate concerns relating to ever-greening of unviable assets.

The operationalization was kicked off for accounts with aggregate exposure to the banking system of larger than ₹20 billion. The exposure threshold would be brought down gradually along a calibrated path over a period of two years to: (i) give stakeholders time to adjust; and (ii) enable the IBC infrastructure to instal in parallel the required capacity to handle more cases. It must be emphasized that the IBC itself is a resolution framework, whereby such accounts will get a lengthy timeframe to be worked out.

8.1 It is helpful to underscore that under the revised framework:

The 8th R: Reset and Ring-Fence to Cement the Change

A. Change of ownership was being favoured even prior to the IBC reference as it leads to assets being classified as standard (as under the earlier schemes). The defaulting promoters also risk losing control of the firm under the IBC bidding. The revised framework would engender incentives for judicious borrowing and to manage better the various business risks that might lead to default.

B. There will also be greater incentive for lenders to implement an efficient turnaround plan to get a quicker upgrade in case of restructuring. Further, since there is no forbearance for assets classified as NPAs, the revised framework will encourage banks to reduce slippages to NPAs through early recognition of stress and timely action, possibly much before a borrower gets into financial difficulty.

The objective was to put in place a predictable, time-compliant process. The IBC, and the RBI's revised framework, helped break the promoter–bank nexus, which has time and again led to crony capitalism and attendant NPA/credit misallocation predicaments as ever-greening and gold-plating suited assorted borrowers and some lenders under the earlier policy and regulatory milieu.

8.2 Finally, the revised framework specifically excluded, from its ambit, micro, small and medium enterprises (MSMEs) with exposures of up to ₹250 million; their revival and rehabilitation were grandfathered and continue to be covered under the earlier norms that were put in place in 2016.

The regulator's conviction was that this was precisely the fundamental reform needed in order to strengthen the credit culture at origination, default, asset quality recognition and resolution stages. By doing so it should weaken, in the first place, opportunities for engaging in frauds relating to loan advances. It was a step that would have helped in the 'ease of doing business' metric, particularly in respect of the *enforcement of contracts* component, where India ranks 163 out of 190; after all, a bank loan is a contract with a borrower. It gave freedom to banks – the only criterion was that there should be a viable restructuring, rated/accredited by a rating agency, within six months. Only after that was the NCLT compulsorily required to be in the picture for recovery, where a *further* 270 (180 + 90) days are allowed before liquidation kicks in. Critics have deemed fifteen months as inadequate and impractical!

The aftermath of the aforementioned initiatives seemed to indicate that they led to a fall in NPA slippages, which is possible evidence of borrowers' concern of instantly being flagged as defaulters; possibly a deterrence effect at work. There was an increase in the closure rate and in Corporate Insolvency Resolution Process (CIRP) admissions after issuance of February 2018 regulations (see Chart 8.1).

Ring-fence the Problem – Prompt Corrective Action

The RBI over the years has worked towards a blueprint to alleviate, if not set aside, concerns over sector stability. The Prompt Corrective Action (PCA), under which specific regulatory actions are taken by the RBI if banks underperform on key operational

The 8th R: Reset and Ring-Fence to Cement the Change

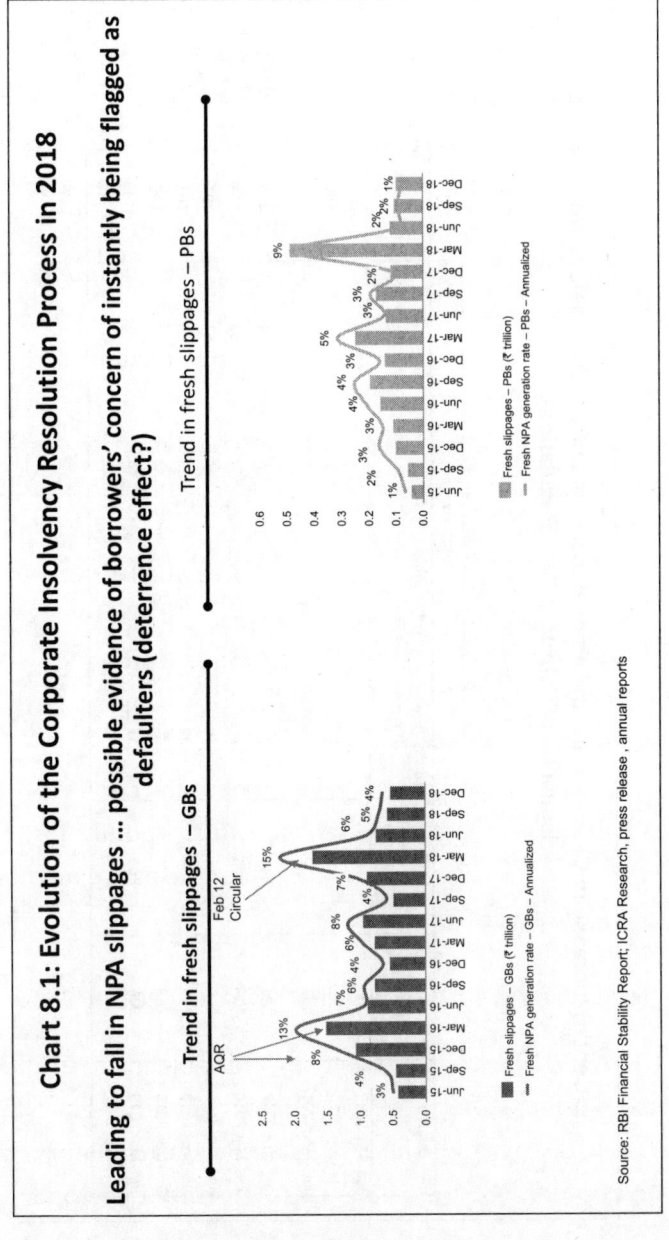

Chart 8.1: Evolution of the Corporate Insolvency Resolution Process in 2018

Leading to fall in NPA slippages ... possible evidence of borrowers' concern of instantly being flagged as defaulters (deterrence effect?)

Source: RBI Financial Stability Report; ICRA Research, press release, annual reports

...(Cont'd) Increase in Closure Rate and Modest Increase in CIRP Admissions Noticed After Issuance of February 2018 Regulations

Quarter	CIRPs at the Beginning of the Quarter	Admitted	Closure by				CIRPs at the End of the Quarter	
			Appeal/ Review/ Settled	Withdrawal under Section 12A	Approval of Resolution Plan*	Commencement of Liquidation		
Jan–Mar 2017	0	37	1	0	0	0	36	
Apr–Jun 2017	36	129	8	0	0	0	157	
July–Sept 2017	157	232	18	0	2	8	361	
Oct–Dec 2017	361	147	38	0	7	24	439	Quarter of introduction of February circular
Jan–Mar 2018	439	195	20	0	11	59	544	
Apr–Jun 2018	544	246	20	1	14	51	704	
Jul–Sept 2018	704	238	29	27	32	86	768	
Oct–Dec 2018	768	275	7	36	14	77	909	
Jan–Mar 2019	909	359	11	27	14	73	1143	
Total		1858	152	91	94	378	1143	

variables, is the most important macro-prudential instrument. The PCA ensures timely supervisory action in case of problem banks; the motivation and design are to strengthen a lender's fundamentals and, at the least, prevent further deterioration from the steady state. Preservation of capital is a key objective.

The PCA rule book, comparable, amongst others, to the US Federal Reserve's framework, incorporates *prudent risk-tolerance* thresholds; it was implemented rigorously (which is meant to say, in letter and spirit) in 2017 to 2018 to help with the convalescence of loss-making GBs and to mitigate the likelihood of an escalation of the problem and balance sheet stress (that is minimize, if not forestall, broader disruption). The proximate goal has been to instil confidence in the wider system – that the regulator is keeping a close watch on financial parameters, including the basic one of profitability.

PCA banks are poorly run. For some of them, the NPAs are a multiple of the sector average even when lending has been partially de-risked because of government policy; for example, loans to the affordable housing segment. To prevent escalation, diminish spillover and avert expansion of the problem, eleven badly performing GBs were placed under the PCA as trigger points were breached. Restrictions were imposed on exposures that intrinsically carried relatively high risk, banks were discouraged from expanding on a risk-weighted asset basis, and other housekeeping strictures such as reducing costs and limits on expensive deposits were imposed.

9

THE EMPIRE STRIKES BACK

Vacillation Has Set In; Discretion and Uncertainty Are Back

IN EARLY 2019, CRITERIA were relaxed to 'graduate' five loss-making banks out of the PCA. Recapitalization of these PCA banks helped them meet the criterion on net NPAs.[1] Hardly anyone disagreed that this was to facilitate higher credit growth. In addition, extension and augmentation of forbearance for MSME loans was granted at the same time. At the upper end of this forbearance (loans of ₹250 million), businesses with annual turnover of up to several hundred crores are beneficiaries. How

---

1   That is, not more than 6 per cent.

does this square up with fairness in a country where the average per capita annual GDP is about ₹150,000?

'RBI's emphasis must be to raise lending and monitoring standards, not launch a loan bonanza, risking another round of bad debts.' Swaminathan A. Aiyar, *Times of India*, 16 December 2018.[2]

The disposition with respect to the IBC or, more generally, in the conviction in the pathway, perceptibly changed – conceivably on defensible grounds – in mid-2018. Instead of buttressing and future-proofing the gains thus far, an atmosphere to go easy on the pedal ensued. A case of our old failing of a premature pronouncement of victory, perhaps? Until then, for the most part, the finance minister and I were on the same page, with frequent conversations on enhancing the landmark legislation's operational efficiency; we sought feedback on changes to preserve the principles that formed the bedrock of the IBC; which tweaks were likely to work; and where resource improvements could help; etc. I suspect the government may have felt that the *deterrence* effect – 'future defaulters beware, you may lose your business' – of the IBC had been achieved, and resolute follow-up to help complete the task was, therefore, unwarranted. But deterrence works only if defaulters – current and potential – face economic consequences within a (reasonable) timeframe; otherwise we are in danger of a relapse to the days of the discredited Securitisation and Reconstruction of

---

[2] Now was the time to 'flood the economy with plentiful cheap credit' with GBs, including the PCA banks, although bank credit had been growing at 15 per cent during the year.

Financial Assets and Enforcement of Security Interest Act, 2002 (SARFAESI) and Recovery of Debts Due to Banks and Financial Institutions Act, 1993 (RDDBFI; DRT for short).

There were requests for rolling back the February circular. A canard was spread that MSMEs would especially suffer, when, in fact, the previous dispensations for this class of borrowers had been explicitly protected in the new regulations. As explained in Chapter 8, the IAC, comprising the RBI's central board members, was keen that a rule-based steady-state process be put in place for directing banks on large NPAs. The risk was that the approach that the IAC/RBI had followed until then might be perceived as ad hoc and subject to legal challenge on grounds of fairness, level playing field and principle of natural justice from those corporate defaulters that had already been referred by the regulator to banks for recovery/liquidation under the aegis of the NCLT. To put it simply, the forty-one largest defaulting promoters could rightly say, 'What about other (large) defaulters?'

Talk of privileges and packages for specific sectors had started doing the rounds; government and other groups were constituted with high-sounding terms of reference including, ominously, for settlement outside the IBC. Recall that in a previous decade 'special restructuring' had started with the airline sector; two out of the three airlines from that episode went out of business anyway, and the third one, owned by the government, is only notionally solvent thanks to sovereign guarantees. Sector interests with aggregate exposure of around ₹2 trillion started a legal onslaught on the RBI's regulation by filing petitions for stay in multiple high courts around the country.

The government and others in 2018 had pleaded to the RBI that with some more time these borrowers would start repaying their lenders. Around the same time, the real-estate sector was exaggerating the scope of spillover to/from NBFCs; some debt mutual funds that had invested in certain entities in that ecosystem – that eventually faced the threat of insolvency – had started a drumbeat about paucity of liquidity. Housing finance companies that borrowed disproportionately in the commercial paper market to fund long tenor mortgages added to the cacophony. (It is said that liquidity does not clean balance sheets.) The evidence did not match the din.

> It may be mentioned as an aside that bank credit to NBFC sector, where there is perception of inadequate bank credit flow, recorded a growth of 17.1 per cent from March 31, 2018 to September 30, 2018 and a year on year growth of 48.3 per cent as on September 30, 2018 on the back of a strong base… [Overall] [b]ank credit has grown 14.4 per cent year-on-year as at fortnight ended October 12, 2018. (Vishwanathan [2018])[3]

Sowing disorder by confusing issues is a tried-and-trusted, distressingly often successful routine by which stakeholders, official and private, plant the seeds of policy/regulation reversal in India; this has been the case for as long as I can remember. It does not help that few policymakers have the patience to sift the

---

3 'Some Thoughts on Credit Risk and Bank Capital Regulation', Speech by N.S. Vishwanathan delivered at XLRI, Jamshedpur, October 2018.

wheat from the chaff, appreciate intricacies and focus on final outcomes. The prospect of a transparent, time-bound process on autopilot for recovering debt was unsettling.

No high court granted a stay to the assorted petitioners. From July 2018 onwards, the IBC was felt, at least by some lobbies, to be constraining, that is, too strict on borrowers in terms of regulatory timelines and the consequences thereof. Lawyers who had agreed to represent the RBI in the Supreme Court (SC) dropped out at the eleventh hour, literally the night before the hearing. The SC granted a stay and postponed hearings more than once, in effect, until the following year.[4] In April 2019, the SC pronounced the regulation to be illegal.

Striking down the February 2018 circular has made the insolvency regime vulnerable, possibly brittle. The SC's specific ruling in the Dharani Sugars case has cut, at the knees, the Banking Regulation (Amendment) Act, 2017, that empowered the RBI to infuse credibility to the IBC by a rule-based time-bound process. Lawyers categorically maintain that the regulator now cannot direct banks to file any reference to the NCLT under the IBC without the government's concurrence; the majority owner of the banking system will, in effect, determine who is a

---

4 The reference to these matters in the chapter is done with the utmost respect for the judiciary, especially the Hon. Supreme Court. The points are made from the perspective of an economist/banking regulator against the objectives of reinforcing incentives, ensuring a systemic efficient (re)allocation of financial capital, and preserving overall financial stability for the sake of our savers/depositors.

defaulter and who will pose a threat to financial stability. This seems to be incongruent with what the RBI claims:

> Further, wherever necessary, the Reserve Bank will issue directions to banks for initiation of insolvency proceedings against borrowers for specific defaults so that the momentum towards effective resolution remains uncompromised.[5]
>
> In sum, we have said that the powers of the RBI under section 35AA and other sections of the Banking Regulation Act are not in doubt.[6]

It is difficult to fully understand, at least for those of us who are not lawyers, that a transparent rule is untenable, but discretion on a case-by-case approach is kosher. That rule, which was introduced after regulatory empowerment in April 2017, and which brought a number of large defaulters to the NCLT with concomitant change in ownership, has been removed. About ₹1.5 trillion has been recovered by banks from the large cases.

As a sidebar, this brings into question how the regulator will act in a timely, nimble manner to, say, arrest instability now that the IBC has been amended to include, against sound principles, defaulting NBFCs as entities that could be referenced to the NCLT.

---

5 Source: https://www.rbi.org.in/Scripts/BS_SpeechesView.aspx?Id=1075, 8 June 2019

6 Source: https://rbidocs.rbi.org.in/rdocs/Content/PDFs/RBIANALYST 04APRILE981CB38C4C44 BA6B4F5A2013 CC9E0B5.PDF, 4 April 2019

A Further Ricochet

The change of mood inevitably percolated to the third stakeholder, viz., the regulator. The RBI's 7 June 2019 regulation, its revised position in place of the February 2018 circular, declared illegal, in effect changed the definition of what constitutes default (for setting in motion steps to be taken by banks) by allowing for a thirty-day 'review' period from the day of missing a debt service payment.[7] The Supreme Court had *not* found the one-day default problematic (as alluded above, it in fact brought the Central bank's regulations in line with the letter and spirit of the IBC) but the June 2019 circular diluted this aspect. A course, reminiscent of the erstwhile mindset of regulatory flexibility, one-time settlement etc., may have been ushered in.

Complexity and confusion were injected. The regulator formally introduced the option of using an inter-creditor agreement as the basis for resolution outside the IBC/NCLT; this had been mooted in 2018 by an ad hoc group. It may turn out to be the latest example of a *trapdoor* to perpetuate squatter rights of defaulters.[8]

---

[7] https://rbidocs.rbi.org.in/rdocs/notification/PDFs/PRUDENTIAL B20DA810F3E148 B099C113C2457FBF8C.PDF

[8] Some readers may find the structure familiar; after all, it can be interpreted as a case of old wine in new bottles under the pretence of 'coordinated' (in)action.

The Empire Strikes Back

Since the SC had held that a transparent general rule[9] with regard to compulsory reference to the IBC was untenable, couldn't the RBI have reverted to issue directions regarding insolvency to banks on a case-by-case approach that it had implemented in 2017 under the guidance of the IAC? After all, the regulator has publicly claimed that the SC judgment does not dilute its powers to '…issue directions to banks for initiation of insolvency proceedings against borrowers for specific defaults…'[10] A list of those defaulters could have been communicated to the banks in the same manner as the first and second lists in June and September 2017, respectively.[11] Had the RBI *chosen* not to direct banks to file cases for resolution of large defaults, which it could do after the 2017 Amendment of the BR Act '…so that the momentum towards effective resolution remains uncompromised'?[12]

More reverberations: return to the twilight zone?

The change in mood is not imagined. It is noteworthy that in late 2019 officials suggested, if not encouraged, that action with respect to defaulters/NPA resolution should be (ideally?) pursued *outside* the IBC.

---

9 Initially for defaulters with outstanding loans of ₹20 billion and above.

10 Source: https://www.rbi.org.in/Scripts/BS_SpeechesView.aspx?Id=1075, 8 June 2019

11 In June for individual NPAs of ₹50 billion and above, and in September for exposure of at least ₹30 billion.

12 Source: https://www.rbi.org.in/Scripts/BS_SpeechesView.aspx?Id=1075, 8 June 2019

'I would therefore request bankers to try to resolve stressed assets in the right earnest and refer cases to NCLT only if satisfied resolution outside the NCLT is not available. We should not use NCLT for every case. This is going to help the business community, banks as well.' – Ministry of Finance, annual general meeting of the Indian Banks' Association.[13]

'Bankruptcy code should not be the first resort for a lender for handling a default, especially in the case of micro, small and medium enterprises (MSMEs). Some changes will be built into the code to ensure that. The government is cognizant of the abuse of the IBC.' – Unnamed government official.[14]

If resolution outside the IBC is the preferred mode, then is the code a fifth wheel at best? Amendments to the BR Act and RBI regulations during the course of 2017 and early 2018 were introduced to arrest the loss of credibility of the code, since lenders left to their devices had opted not to deploy the law to resolve NPAs.

There is a risk of these developments going from mere distraction to a dangerous sideshow. The spiral of delays,

---

13 Source: https://www.livemint.com/industry/banking/do-not-use-insolvency-code-for-every-stressed-asset-junior-fm-anurag-thakur-1568200593817.html, 11 September 2019.

14 Source: https://www.livemint.com/industry/banking/govt-to-check-lenders-use-of-ibc-over-minor-delays-in-repayments-11570988853947.html, 13 October 2019.

characteristic of the not-too-distant past, may already be upon us. Regarding stressed accounts with exposure of at least ₹20 billion, a banker, days before the six-month resolution plan window under the June 2019 circular was coming to an end, said: 'The framework is all right. What we feel is it is difficult to resolve a company within six–seven months. So, for the inter-credit agreement [ICA] to function properly, at least nine–ten months should be given.'[15]

Predictably, the bankers' accord, proposed as a staging post, has become a destination. Lenders already have had a lot longer than 'nine–ten months'. Despite twenty-one months, from February 2018 to June 2019, plus six more months up to January 2020 to resolve, progress, reportedly, has been underwhelming.

The government amended the IBC for the third time in July 2019; in this instance a valid, albeit belated, attempt on a stakeholder, viz., the judiciary, to curb delays by mandating a hard 330-day limit for the NCLT process on the resolution professional and the adjudicating authority, including litigation, from the earlier 270 days. Was this perceived as feeble and maybe lacking in conviction, as the RBI's February 2018 circular had been issued to impose discipline on stakeholders, which the government was very keen to have set aside? Possibly, the irony was not lost.

The SC in November 2019 relaxed/removed the mandatory limit under Article 19(1)(g) of the Constitution, saying that

---

15 Source: 'We've Seen Healthy Growth in Term Loans', *Business Standard*, 2 January 2020.

the amendment was an excessive and unreasonable restriction on the litigant's right to carry business.[16] The amendment was deemed to be incongruous with Article 14, which says that the state cannot deny to any person equality before the law or equal protection of the laws within India. One implication is that since lenders have hardly exhibited alacrity in expeditiously initiating and concluding matters under the IBC, an open-ended process is now perhaps the settled outcome. Every timeline will be justified under some circumstance or the other. While the litigant's right to carry business is reasonable and justified, shouldn't it also be balanced against the obvious *externality*, viz., the bank's right to carry business, since delay/non-recovery of dues directly impinges on how much capital a bank gains, saves and loses, which in turn determines whether and how much it can lend, that is, conduct its business? Second, it also has an impact on the business prospects of operational creditors, as delay in repayment of their dues, even partial, can, in fact, drive some of them out of business altogether. Third, delays add to the build-up towards sector instability, which is where we were in 2014.

Any verdict that entails optimization over an objective without a *constraint* (in this instance, the impact on other stakeholders) often leads to 'corner' outcomes; an inevitable corollary of a bifocal judgment, which accepts one valid argument and virtually discounts all other considerations; in this instance in perpetuity,

---

16 For a lucid explanation of some of these points, see the excellent article: Sanjeev Nayyar, 'Constitutional Issues Arising from Telecom, Essar Rulings', *Financial Express*, 21 November 2019.

or until a 'final' judgment comes about. The back-and-forth alluded above need not end even then.

Subsequent to an SC judgment in early 2019, the NCLAT passed an order in July, which was finally decided in November. It would seem that finality rests only with the highest court. Moreover, what about the time value of money, which is the essence of banking? Surely, in a commercial matter, a pecuniary amount has to be assessed for an important economic concept that is at the heart of lending and borrowing? Further, there is inequity; only corporate litigants with deep pockets can afford litigation in excess of 800 days (see Appendix 2 for timeline and associated decision nodes for one particular case).

The legal/administration process is again caught in a cleft stick of: (i) *externality-agnostic* objectives, where implications for other stakeholders, let alone economic welfare, are ignored; and (ii) *outcome-agnostic* incentives of GBs, despite the clear and strong legal recourse on offer. The restraining effect of the IBC may get compromised, and the behavioural change may not last long (SARFAESI and DRT suffered that fate.) The justice system has not helped to draw a line under a commercial dispute in a timely manner and curbed a regulator to do so in a rule-based transparent way.

The distinct possibility that promoters/sponsors would lose ownership rights over their defaulting businesses, which had reset incentives for timely debt servicing, has receded – to what degree, time will tell. The likelihood that jobs are saved on a *durable* basis is higher when there is a greater chance that a business will continue as a going concern under different proprietors than when it is allowed to be driven into the ground by defaulting extant owners, which is more likely to happen when decisions are delayed interminably.

Since the time-bound threat of an insolvency application is not credible anymore, it is unclear what threat points will compel resolution in 180 days (or, for that matter, even 365 days). Banks will have to set aside capital under the June 2019 regulation if a resolution is not in place in 180 days and then in 365 days after the review period.[17] In sum, there are no hard consequences for errant borrowers as compulsory recovery/liquidation is off the table or, for that matter, for GBs, since remuneration of bank staff is unaffected. Banks will make provisions, book lower profits and write off capital as living-dead borrowers stay afloat.

The June 2019 regulation is *time-inconsistent* if the goal is efficient resolution and recovery. Economic consequences for higher provision by GBs, touted as a disincentive by the regulator, will be felt only by taxpayers, as more money will have to be coughed up by the exchequer to shore up the quantum of uncompromised capital. Even larger fines by the regulator on GBs are futile under these circumstances – employment terms and conditions in government-owned institutions see to it.

The banks which got cover from the regulator for invoking the NCLT are now again exposed to the same influences/factors that had dissuaded them from using the IBC's recovery/liquidation provisions after it came into law in 2016, but remained dormant, at least in respect of large corporate loans. Taking away the discretion (after 180 days of flexibility for designing a resolution

---

17 January 2020 and July 2020.

plan) with a fixed timeline process meant that the second-guessing of banks' commercial evaluation was difficult to justify by the investigative agencies. Taking decisions on haircuts, etc., under the ambit of the February 2018 circular, would have been easier for bank management.

The previous paragraphs were written in November 2019, before the 210-day period for resolution was over under the regulator's June 2019 regulation. The assessment, in early January 2020, reported in the media (quoting a source) makes for sobering if predictable reading: 'The RBI's internal review of 13 banks' stressed assets initially assigned under its June 7 circular—of ₹20 billion and above—notes that an ICA is yet to be signed for exposures amounting to ₹336.1 billion while the same has been signed with respect to aggregate exposures of ₹60.75 billion. And resolution plans have been implemented only with respect to one borrower with a reported exposure of ₹16.17 billion.'[18]

The same report also says that the 'Central bank is, in particular, concerned about the huge increase in frauds; and whether a cover-up may be the reason for the lack of movement under the June 7 [2019] circular, as also the collapse of the ICA.'

Numbers back the commentary. The latest documents on the state of banks, the Financial Stability Report and Report on Trend and Progress of Banking in India [December 2019], inform that the value of frauds of ₹5 billion and above in the first half of 2019/20 jumped to ₹1.1 trillion from ₹617.6 billion in 2018/19.

---

18 'Banks, Bankers May Face Fines for Poor Progress Over RBI's June 7 Circular', *Business Standard,* 14 January 2020

10

OUTCOMES AND IMPLICATIONS OF THE RS

THE CONCERNS OVER FINANCIAL stability were put to rest to a considerable extent; capital levels in most banks as of 2019 are comfortable. This was perhaps *the* overriding checkbox, and a worthy achievement of the authorities post 2014. It could be that the Indian lending model is gradually and grudgingly becoming more discerning now. Sections of the Indian corporate sector had to deleverage and measurable progress has been made in this regard. On the other hand, the cost, beyond the obvious pecuniary one, has not been inconsiderable. Reputations have suffered.[1] After a length of time, balance sheets of banks are now, for the most part, more accurate.

Indicative of ratios for 2019, there has been a decline in GNPAs of GBs compared to March 2018, but the ratio is higher compared to March 2017.[2][3] Due to the government's capital contribution – taxpayers walked the talk – net NPAs at the sector level, taking into account the provision coverage ratio, have declined appreciably from 7.4 per cent in March 2017 to 5.1 per cent in September 2019.

The multi-pronged approach described above is an ongoing process. The early signs are, on balance, not discouraging. While the IBC has gained modest traction in the last couple of years as an instrument for banks to salvage money from NPAs, progress is patchy. The slow progress may suggest that it is a visible sign of gaming; the average resolution time has been over 350 days, going up to 800 days in at least one high-profile case.[4] While the IBC was structured as a single-window mechanism for resolution/insolvency, it quickly morphed in practice into a

---

1 For example, even the largest lender received recap funding from the government in 2018.

2 Note that the data cited is from the RBI's Financial Stability Report (various issues since December 2018). Between March and September 2019, the GNPA ratio for GBs marginally *increased*.

3 A word of caution on the task of the repair still left: there are banks whose NPAs, including write-offs, are at 10–30 per cent.

4 By some measures, the pace of resolution has slowed and the average, reportedly, is about 500 days. ('India Corporate Health Tracker, 3Q20: Telecom in Focus' Credit Suisse, 25 February 2020)

ping-pong between three legal windows, the National Company Law Tribunal (NCLT), the National Company Law Appellate Tribunal (NCLAT) and the Supreme Court. It is hoped that the IBC process itself will evolve as the case history of various NCLT and NCLAT judgments builds up.

So far, resolution of sizeable corporate defaulters has been limited. Nevertheless, large borrowers for the first time felt the heat as several of the first twelve accounts directed to the NCLT acquired new owners. During 2018/19, financial creditors recovered about 43 per cent of the ₹3.5 trillion claimed under the IBC; much of the recovery has been from large accounts. The percentage represents a significant improvement compared to previous years. The recovery percentage had actually been declining – for illustration, 18 per cent in 2013/14 down from 31 per cent in 2010/11.

At a broader level, the shrinking autonomy of GBs and an inevitably prolonged (contingent) fiscal commitment from the government to the banking sector are major casualties of this latest cycle of NPA escalation that had its seeds planted in the early to mid-2010s. The government's priorities in terms of lending to specific segments – say, MSME and agriculture – and bailing out systemic sectors like power generation have been perceived to be undermined by the RBI's rules on default definition and by GBs placed under the PCA framework. Consequently, the regulator's de facto powers have been diluted on several subjects related to, inter alia, preserving financial stability. Circulars were reversed and the PCA framework essentially ditched as these came in the way of stimulating the economy through higher credit growth.

As recently as the third quarter of 2019/20, some large GBs reported losses; perhaps this is expected. What is cause for concern is that in October and December 2019 ten banks (of which nine were GBs) disclosed that for the previous financial year the regulator, upon inspection, had found their NPAs to be higher than reported a few months prior in the annual financial accounts. A back-of-the-envelope calculation implies that the GNPA ratio for GBs could be about 0.3 per cent higher than the estimate reported for end March 2019.[5] This would indicate that there is lingering scope for being conservative with the truth, which observers felt had been left behind after the AQR.

Virtually no equity for GBs was raised from the capital market – non-government and ex-LIC. The capital market requirement for listing, viz., a minimum 15 per cent of free float for entities listed in the stock market, has been blithely ignored for GBs. There has been little divestment by GBs of joint ventures, special purpose vehicles and asset management companies despite Indian share markets, overall, remaining quite buoyant over the last two years until February 2020. There is no evidence of appetite for selling shares by the principal owner, even when post stake sale the government will continue to be the majority owner.

Sector consolidation – cited as a reform measure – was initiated in 2018. Three GBs were merged, which, going by past experience, usually leads to erosion in value, over time, of the entity that takes over the weaker ones. In 2020, a further ten GBs

---

5 The aggregate increase in GNPAs for the ten banks was ₹265 billion, of which 45 per cent was accounted by the largest GB.

were merged into four.[6] One highly problematic GB was taken over by the wholly government-owned LIC, possibly contrary to sound and widely accepted investment conventions, as also on grounds of contributing to systemic risk.

Large fines and strictures on banks have been imposed for underreporting NPAs, accounting fudges and regulatory violations, more generally (see Chart 10.1). As mentioned earlier, banks in December 2019 have had to reveal bookkeeping discrepancies and restate balance-sheet figures. This casts doubt on the effectiveness of penalties imposed by the regulator. Frankly, the *flow of funds* in the case of GBs suggests that monetary penalties are a case of money going from the 'left pocket' to the 'right pocket' (money collected by the RBI is passed on to the government as surplus), and back to the 'left pocket' (government returns the money to GBs for recapitalization).

Implications

It is possible that episodic high-risk perceptions for the sector will likely persist inter alia due to:

1. The government's budgetary considerations; an intermittent start–stop approach to injecting capital may continue. Market perception is that the principal owner is

---

6 Since management time is taken up by HR and system reconciliation challenges, business (credit) growth of the merged entity usually suffers.

Outcomes and Implications of the Rs

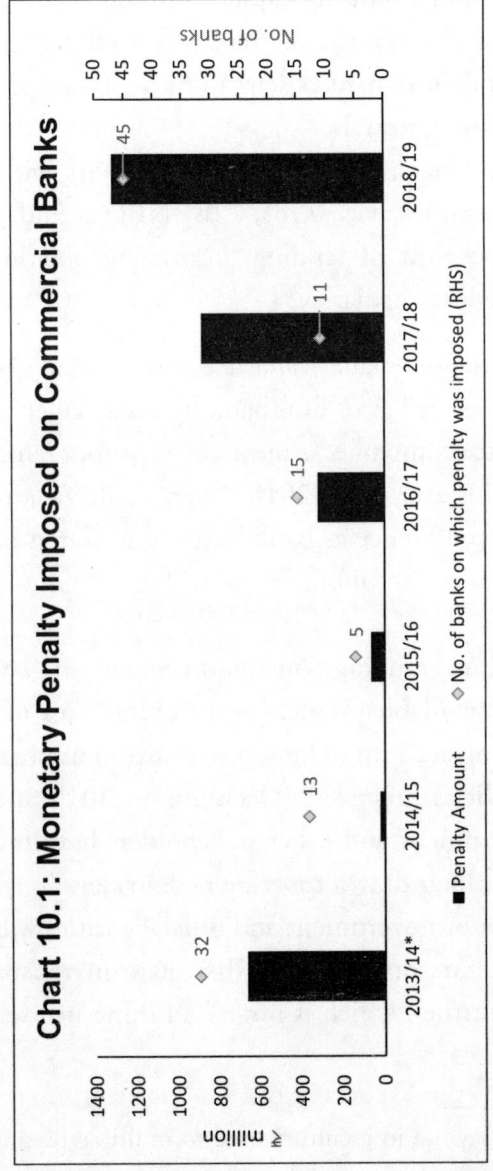

Source: RBI Annual Report 2018–19.

one step behind regarding capital infusion into its banks due to fiscal constraints; matters may well accentuate if government debt dynamics start to move unfavourably on account of lower growth.
2. Interconnectedness, encompassing complexity within and between categories, viz., GBs, PBs, NBFCs and mutual funds, on account of lending, borrowing and investing amongst the intermediaries.

An AQR exercise for smaller value accounts in banks (such as loans to MSMEs) as well as of non-banking financial companies and housing finance companies is inevitable; without fanfare, the RBI had started this exercise in 2018. There could be attendant consequences for confidence as banks' exposure to non-banking financial companies was about ₹6.5 trillion at the end of March 2019.

India's very low ranking on enforcement of contracts compared to commendable progress in the overall 'ease of doing' ranking is mainly on account of long gestation and unpredictable administrative-judicial practices.[7] Decisions in 2019 and early 2020 by the government and other stakeholders have increased the likelihood that long-drawn cases are here to stay.

Periodic bailout by government and official entities will likely continue, at least for some banks. GBs' share in the banking sector will erode further, which is not a bad thing in itself from

---

7 There is an old saying: in a culture used to multiple lifetimes, the time value of money is immaterial.

an efficiency perspective, in particular of capital deployed. There is little likelihood of significant operational improvement. For instance, HR right-sizing to increase productivity is not possible on account of the state's objective of preserving economic privileges of employees irrespective of profitability.

For private banks, strong regulation and market discipline will, for the most part, be sufficient as guardrails. They will likely remain out of trouble, and raise risk capital from markets, including equity from foreign investors.

Time will tell, in the aftermath of the setting aside of the February 2018 regulation, whether 'extend and pretend' will make a comeback under the aegis of the RBI's new rules and, possibly, official preference for resolution outside the IBC/NCLT, as also relaxing the definition of default.

We didn't have to wait long for the 'camel's nose to appear under the tent'.[8] Forbearance to the commercial real estate was granted in February 2020. For the regulator, direction from the government to acquiesce to forbearance requests, especially during periods when stimulating the economy becomes the focus for policymakers, may continue. Specifically, dilution of asset recognition norms for sectors, viz., MSMEs (continuously since

---

8 'A camel's nose under the tent'. Explanation: A small, seemingly innocuous act or decision that will lead to much larger, more serious and less desirable consequences down the line. The term refers to an alleged Arab proverb that if a camel is allowed to get its nose inside a tent, it will be impossible to prevent the rest of it from entering. Source: https://idioms.thefreedictionary.com

2016 for some categories even as the NPA ratio is 8.7–11.5 per cent), infrastructure through wing-and-a-prayer restructuring, etc., is not ruled out.

As the fiscal constraint becomes more acute, a downward revision of the mandatory capital to risk-weighted assets ratio (CRAR), which is currently commensurate with extant risks (credit rating inflation in India) could be inadvisably contemplated. As it is, the provision coverage ratio still falls short when compared to average recoveries of NPAs through resolution and liquidation.

11

THE 9TH R: REFORM – GONE AWOL[1][2]

Banking Regulatory Powers Should Be Ownership-Neutral

THIS CHAPTER SEEKS TO highlight some fundamental fissures that exist in the regulation of banks, in particular GBs. The aftermath of the large fraud that came to light in early

---

1 This chapter is an edited version of the Inaugural Lecture at the Centre for Law & Economics, Centre for Banking & Financial Laws, Gujarat National Law University, Gandhinagar, March 2018.
2 AWOL translates into 'absent without leave', meaning disappeared or untraceable.

2018 provides the backdrop.³ There was the usual blame game, passing the buck and a tonne of honking, mostly short-term and knee-jerk reactions. These prevented the participants in this cacophony from the deep reflection and soul searching that can help solve fundamental issues, which are the root cause of such frauds and related irregularities in the banking sector and, as I will explain, are in fact far too regular.

Let me start with the Reserve Bank's supervision of banks, which has been commented upon.

IMF/World Bank FSAP assessment

In its 2017 Financial Sector Assessment Programme (FSAP) of India, conducted, completed and released prior to the episode of fraud that came to light in early 2018, the International Monetary Fund (IMF) and the World Bank (WB) made the following observations:

1. In the publicly released FSSA (Financial System Stability Assessment) report:⁴

The RBI has made substantial progress in strengthening banking supervision:

A key achievement was the introduction in 2013 of risk-based supervision through a comprehensive and forward-

---

3 Media reports in late 2019, ostensibly based on forensic audits, suggest that the quantum of funds involved is even larger.
4 Page 17, para 35

looking Supervisory Program for Assessment of Risk and Capital (SPARC). The Basel III framework and other international guidance were implemented or are being phased in, including stricter regulations on large exposures. Domestic and cross-border cooperation arrangements are now firmly in place. The AQR [Asset Quality Review] and the strengthening of regulations in 2015 have improved distressed asset recognition. In April 2017, the RBI established a new Enforcement Department and revised its prompt corrective action framework to incorporate more prudent risk-tolerance thresholds [that is updated, commensurate with extant sector hazard].

2. Further, in its specific comments on Other Regulation, Accounting, and Disclosure:[5]

The internal control regulations issued by the RBI are adequate and are supported by the requirements of the SPARC risk-based supervision system. This system provides extensive guidelines for inspection of the internal control and audit function, and prescribes that a bank's internal controls allow identification and controlling of risks. The Internal Audit Departments in banks are required to have appropriate resources and staff with the requisite skills. Tasks can be outsourced, allowing additional expertise to be brought in. The auditors reported that overall experience with the quality of internal audit of banks was satisfactory.

---

5 Core Principles or CPs 20, 26–29, page 21, para 60.

However, the FSAP of India laments, at several points, the fact that the Reserve Bank's regulatory powers over banks are not neutral to bank ownership:

1. In the Detailed Assessment Report (DAR) on the Basel Core Principles (BCP) on Effective Banking Supervision:[6]

Some previously observed weaknesses concerning the independence of the RBI and the inherent conflict of interest when supervising government-owned banks (GBs) remain. The RBI enjoys a large degree of operational autonomy, but amendments to several legal provisions, and formal grounding of RBI independence in the RBI Act, would provide greater legal certainty. The RBI's legal powers to supervise and regulate GBs are also constrained – it cannot remove GB directors or management, who are appointed by the government of India (GoI), nor can it force a merger or trigger the liquidation of a GB; it[RBI] has also limited legal authority to hold GB Boards accountable regarding strategic direction, risk profiles, assessment of management, and compensation. Legal reforms are thus highly desirable to empower the RBI to fully exercise the same responsibilities for GBs as now apply to private banks, and to ensure a level playing field in supervisory enforcement.

---

6 Page 7, para 6

The 9th R: Reform – Gone AWOL

2. Specifically, on corporate governance:[7]

The appropriate rules on fitness and propriety, and banks' internal governance structures, are in place with respect to private and foreign banks. Nevertheless, the influence the RBI may exercise on banks' governance through section 21 BR Act, placement of RBI representatives on banks' Boards, and the RBI's very limited authority under the Banking Acts, as well as the custom to hold the GB Boards accountable has become problematic. Under the law and according to custom, the RBI cannot hold GB Boards accountable for assessing and – when necessary – replacing weak and nonperforming senior management and government-appointed Board members.[8]

---

7 CP 14, page 18, para 50

8 It is to be noted here that the FSAP also mentions in Other Regulation, Accounting and Disclosure (CPs 20, 26–29, page 21, para 62):

> Currently, the external auditor is not obliged to report immediately to the RBI regulator any issues encountered in the audited bank that are of material interest to the supervisor. This is only permitted after publication of the annual statements. Moreover, regulators need powers to access the auditor's working papers when needed. This is currently not envisaged. The laws and/or regulations should explicitly authorize the external auditor to inform the RBI of any concerns at any time; also, before the annual statements have been finalized and published. The RBI should be given the explicit authority to obtain information at any time from the external auditor.

This point, however, applies for both GBs and PBs.

Banking Regulatory Powers in India Are NOT Ownership Neutral

All commercial banks in India are regulated by the RBI under the Banking Regulation (BR) Act of 1949. Additionally, all GBs are regulated by the GoI under the Banking Companies (Acquisition and Transfer of Undertakings) Act, 1970; the Bank Nationalization Act, 1980; and the State Bank of India Act, 1955. Section 51 of the amended BR Act explicitly states which portions of the BR Act apply to the GBs, most common thread across the *omissions* being complete removal or emaciation of RBI powers on corporate governance at GBs:

1. The RBI cannot remove directors and management at GBs as Section 36AA (1) of the BR Act is not applicable to the GBs.
2. Section 36ACA (1) of the BR Act that provides for supersession of a bank board is also not applicable in the case of GBs (and regional rural banks or RRBs) as they are not banking companies registered under the Companies Act.
3. Section 10B (6) of the BR Act that provides for removal of the chairman and managing director of a banking company is not operative in the case of GBs.[9]
4. The RBI cannot force a merger in the case of GBs as per Section 45 of the BR Act.

---

9 The exception to this is IDBI Bank Ltd for which the Articles of Association (Clause 120) grants the RBI the requisite authority.

5. GB's banking activity does not require a licence from the RBI under Section 21 of the BR Act; hence, the RBI cannot revoke a licence under Section 22 (4) of the BR Act as it can in the case of private sector banks.
6. The RBI cannot trigger liquidation of GBs as per Section 39 of the BR Act.
7. Furthermore, in a remarkable exception of sorts, in some cases there is duality of managing director and the chairman – they are the same – implying that the managing director is primarily answerable only to himself or herself!

This legislative reality has in effect led to a deep fissure in the landscape of banking regulatory terrain: a system of dual regulation, by the finance ministry in addition to the RBI.[10] This fissure or fault line is bound to lead to tremors.

The temptation to engage in fraud at the level of employee or employees is always present, in banks (or in corporations), be it in the public sector or private sector. The question, then, is whether there is adequate deterrence faced by employees from undertaking frauds and enough incentives for management to put in place preventive measures to pre-empt frauds, which is

---

10 Of course, there are several other (well-documented) implications of being GBs: board constitution, wherein it is difficult to categorize any director as independent; significant and widening compensation differences with private sector banks, leading to the erosion of specialized skills; external vigilance enforcement though the Central Vigilance Commission and Central Bureau of Investigation; and limited applicability of the Right to Information Act.

an *operational* risk. In case of banks, three potentially powerful mechanisms could induce discipline against frauds:

1. Investigative/vigilance/legal deterrence: Criminal investigation of frauds and attached penalties can serve as an effective deterrence if reporting and investigation are expedient and penalties are adequately severe relative to the gains from fraudulent activity (see Chapter 13).
2. Market discipline: Fraudulent activity can be a net loss to the bottom line; in this case, bank investors would impose deterrence, for example, uninsured creditors might run on the bank inducing liquidity problems, or shareholders might exit, effectively raising the cost of capital and inducing solvency questions. In anticipation of such disruptive outcomes that might cause loss of control, management and board members may put in place governance mechanisms to prevent or reduce the incidence of fraud and/or hold larger buffers in the capital structure to bear losses when fraud materializes.
3. Regulatory discipline: Banks in most parts of the world, however, have a significant portion of deposit funding that is insured, and since banks serve critical payments and settlements function, they are often too big to fail or too many to fail. Hence, a part of the market discipline is weakened as a tradeoff with financial stability and is substituted by delegation of supervisory and regulatory powers to a banking regulator. Detection and punishment by the regulator then need to be effective to discipline fraud.

The 9th R: Reform – Gone AWOL

How do these mechanisms work in case of PBs and GBs in India?

In our country, an investigative and formal enforcement process takes, conceivably for the right reasons, a fair bit of time. Indeed, RBI data on banking frauds suggests that only a handful of cases over the past five years have had closure, and cases of substantive economic significance remain open. As a result, the overall enforcement mechanism – at least until now – is undoubtedly not a deterrent to frauds relative to private economic gains from fraud.

It is fair to say that in case of PBs, the real deterrence is from market and regulatory discipline, and their confluence. A PB chief executive officer's primary concern is whether s/he will be able to raise capital when the need arises, or even whether s/he will still be running the bank the next day. The point is that they could be readily cautioned through their boards and even replaced by the RBI in case of large or persistent irregularities. Further, a PB failing to meet bank solvency standards and under the RBI's Prompt Corrective Action would find it hard to raise capital, whereby it would need to put the house in order at swift notice so that it can raise funding from markets and get back on the growth path. In turn, there are incentives to invest in governance, so as to limit frauds and regulatory violations, and to respond with alacrity when incidents do arise.

In contrast, the market discipline mechanism for GBs is appreciably weaker compared to those for PBs. There is implicitly a stronger perceived sovereign guarantee for all creditors of GBs, and the principal shareholder – the government – has so far not been interested in fundamentally modifying the ownership structure. From an economic viewpoint, this weakened market discipline should imply that the government would prefer *stronger* regulatory discipline of these banks, not *weaker*. However, as explained above, and perhaps since the original idea behind bank nationalization was *complete* government control over credit allocation to the economy, the situation in India is exactly the reverse: the RBI's regulatory powers over GBs are *weaker* than those over the PBs.

The BR Act exemptions for GBs mean that the one agency – the regulatory – that can respond relatively quickly against banking frauds or irregularities cannot take effective action. Hence, for example, managing directors at GBs find it comfortable to tell the media that business will be as usual for them under the RBI's PCA framework, as even if they do not meet the stipulated restrictions of the framework, the ultimate authority over their tenure is with the government and not with the RBI.

It is not entirely surprising that there has been a recurring theme in report after report on financial sector reforms in the country that has suggested strengthening of GB governance through improvement in top management and board member appointments, or ownership neutrality in banking regulatory powers, or by improving market discipline by considering a variety of diverse ownership structures.

The present NPA challenge provided an opportunity to catalyse fundamental reform at GBs. What needs to be done is clear. From the RBI's standpoint, legislative changes to the BR Act that make banking regulatory powers ownership neutral –

not piecemeal, but *fully* – is a minimum requirement. It might also be the most readily feasible of these options.[11]

Why does all this matter?

The potential loss to banks from malpractices that are getting detected and reported has reached epic proportions (see the RBI's Financial Stability Reports from 2018 onwards). The sharp rise since 2016/17 could, in part, be due to frauds committed in the past only being reported now;[12] the pace seems to have picked up (more on this below). The contrast between GBs and PBs with regard to fraud affliction is noteworthy. By value, around 90 per cent of frauds are accounted for by malpractices in GBs.

---

11 The duality of banking regulatory powers exists even in the case of cooperative banks where the RBI has to contend with several powers being vested away from it in the hands of state governments. Cooperative banks are typically small and their failures are dealt adequately with through liquidation by the Deposit Insurance and Credit Guarantee Corporation (DICGC), which insures some of their depositors. This duality also needs to be addressed as part of the broader banking sector reforms to improve credit culture and reduce fraudulent lending.

12 In May 2014 the RBI had directed banks to begin a process of red-flagging accounts that showed signs of fraud; in September 2014 a registry was proposed. Finally, in January 2016, the RBI put in place a Central Fraud Registry, which is a searchable database to help banks detect instances of fraud by borrowers early on. In February 2018, the government directed its banks that all non-performing assets larger than ₹500 million have to be examined for possible fraud.

No Banking Regulator Can Catch or Prevent All Frauds

There has been a tendency in the pronouncements post revelation of the fraud mentioned at the beginning of the chapter that the RBI supervision team should have caught it. While that can always be said ex-post with any fraud, it is simply unfeasible for a banking regulator to be in every nook and corner of banking activity to rule out frauds by 'being there'. If a regulator could achieve such perfect outcomes, it would effectively imply that the regulator can do anything that banks can do and, by implication, can simply perform the entire banking intermediation activity itself. What is needed is for various mechanisms to deter frauds and other irregularities to be in place and have bite so that fraud incidence is low and magnitudes contained. Indeed, frauds have happened at banks in regimes with varied levels of banking regulatory quality and in both public and private banks.

In the specific case at hand, the Reserve Bank had identified, based on cyber risk considerations, the exact source of operational hazard – through which we understand now that the fraud had been perpetrated. In particular, the RBI had issued precise instructions via three circulars in 2016 to enable banks to eliminate the hazard. It turns out ex-post the bank had simply not done so. Clearly, the internal processes at the bank failed in allowing the operational hazard to remain in place in spite of clear instructions to close it. As was stated in the RBI's press statement on the case, this was essentially an *operational* failure at the second largest government-owned bank. The RBI did undertake actions against the bank that it is empowered to, but this set is limited under its BR Act powers over GBs.

Indeed, in an interview to the Press Trust of India on 11 March 2018, the IMF deputy managing director reinforced this point along with others alluded to above:

> [W]e think the GB recapitalization should be part of a broader package of financial reforms to speed up the resolution of NPAs, improve GB governance, reduce the role of the public sector in the financial system, and enhance bank lending capacity and practices… The experts recommended legal changes to enable the RBI to extend all the powers currently exercised over private sector banks to government ones; in particular, regarding board member dismissals, mergers, and licence revocation… Having said that, banks' operational risk management, risk culture, internal control frameworks and external audit function should typically play a central role in preventing fraud.

Need to Refocus on the Bigger Issue of Stressed Assets Resolution

Let me now turn to an issue of greater magnitude and significance than the banking fraud uncovered in 2018. The RBI's Financial Stability Report of June 2017 clarifies that there is a link between bank frauds and the stressed assets problem:[13]

---

13 Section VII: Frauds; Para 3.36

OVERDRAFT

One of the emerging risks to the financial sector is increasing trends in frauds in commercial banks and financial institutions. During the last five financial years, frauds have increased substantially both in volume and value terms. During this period, while the volume of frauds has increased by 19.6 per cent from 4235 to 5064, the value (loss incurred) has increased by 72 per cent from ₹97.5 billion to ₹167.7 billion. Share of frauds in [loan] advances portfolio continued to be high at 86 per cent of the frauds reported during 2016–17 (in terms of amount involved)... In a number of large value frauds, serious gaps in credit underwriting standards were evident. Some of the often-seen gaps are liberal cash flow projection at the proposal stage, lack of continuous monitoring of cash flows and cash profits (EBITDA), lack of security perfection and over valuation, gold plating of projects, diversion of funds, double financing and general credit governance issues in banks. Moreover, almost all corporate-loan-related fraud cases get seasoned for 2 to 3 years as NPAs before they are reported as fraud.

In plain and simple English, these practices amount to a looting of the country's future by some in the business community, in cahoots with some lenders. The RBI also felt the anger, hurt and pain at the banking sector frauds and irregularities. As safeguards of deposits at banks, work began in right earnest in 2015 to cleanse the Augean Stables – ably conducted by supervisory teams and

The 9th R: Reform – Gone AWOL

as acknowledged objectively by experts of reputed multilateral agencies, to break this unholy nexus.

The owner of numerous and large banks – the government – which has provided the landmark IBC, the related ordinances and the bank recapitalization package to get the churn going, might consider making further, equally important contributions and complete the jigsaw by:

1. Making banking regulatory powers neutral to bank ownership and levelling the playing field between GBs and PBs; and,
2. Informing itself about what do with the government part of the banking system going forward as part of optimizing over the best use of scarce national fiscal resources.

C: BITS AND PIECES

12

AGRICULTURE CREDIT[1]

FARM LOAN WAIVERS HAVE been of topical interest. The multidimensional subject has engaged the farming community, policymakers, academics, analysts and researchers. On the one hand, there is a gamut of issues that have intensified the anguish of our farmers. In this context, farm loan waivers have brought forward the urgency of designing lasting solutions to the structural malaise that affects Indian agriculture. On the

---

1 This chapter is based on edited remarks compiled for a seminar on 'Agricultural Debt Waiver – Efficacy and Limitations', Reserve Bank of India, 31 August 2017 (some data has been updated).

other, there are concerns about the macroeconomic and financial implications, how long they will persist in impacting the economy, the possible distortions that they could confront public policies with, and the ultimate incidence of the pecuniary burden.

One can attempt to eclectically address both sides of the debate. India's agrarian economy is the source of around 17 per cent of its GDP, 11 per cent of its exports and provides livelihood to about half of its population. The importance of the sector from a macroeconomic perspective is also reflected in a significant flow of bank credit to finance agricultural and allied activities relative to other sectors of the economy. Outstanding bank advances to agriculture and allied activities have risen from 20 per cent of the GDP originating in agriculture and allied activities in 2000/01 to about 52 per cent in 2017/18 (Chart 12.1), which is slightly higher than the economy-wide bank credit–GDP ratio.

In real terms, adjusted for inflation measured by the GDP deflator, the growth of bank credit to agriculture and allied activities accelerated from 2.5 per cent in the 1990s to around 15 per cent from 2000/01 to 2017/18. Obviously, the 'delta' is considerably above growth of the sector.[2] Is it a case of capital deepening, or have we ended up with a quantum of credit/stock of loans that cannot be serviced, given the value of production? If it's capital deepening, then annual average output increases should have been higher over a period.

---

2 The sector's annual average growth has been about 3.1 per cent (during 2011/12 to 2017/18).

Agriculture Credit

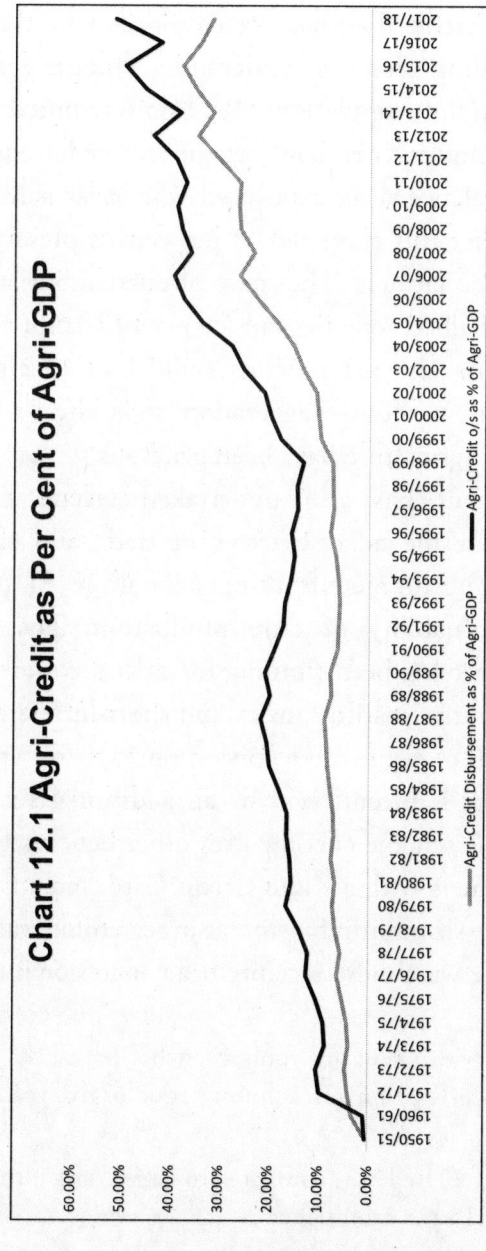

Chart 12.1 Agri-Credit as Per Cent of Agri-GDP

— Agri-Credit Disbursement as % of Agri-GDP
— Agri-Credit o/s as % of Agri-GDP

Source: Report of the Internal Working Group to Review Agricultural Credit, 2019, RBI.

Much of this credit flow has been propelled by the policy thrust on expanding credit to agriculture, especially through priority sector-lending stipulations. Banks are required to lend 18 per cent of annual net bank credit or credit equivalent amounts of off-balance sheet exposures, whichever is higher, to agriculture.[3] Under this carve-out, 8 per cent is prescribed for small and marginal farmers. The share of outstanding advances to agriculture and allied activities in total priority sector advances has increased from 32.5 per cent in 2000/01 to 43.2 per cent in 2016/17. Thus, without exaggeration, it is safe to say that financial flows to agriculture have been generous.[4]

The government has also undertaken several measures to compensate for the adverse terms of trade and the inert institutional architecture confronting agriculture in order to improve the profitability of crop production. The Interest Subvention Scheme has been running for a decade under which banks and cooperative institutions extend short-term crop loans of up to ₹300,000 to farmers at a concessional rate of 7 per cent. Timely repayment is incentivized by an additional subvention of 3 per cent. The scheme encompasses other benefits for small and marginal farmers with a Kisan Credit Card, including post-harvest loans up to six months for storage in accredited warehouses against negotiable warehouse receipts at a concessional rate of 7

---

[3] Foreign banks with twenty or more branches have been required to attain this target within a maximum period of five years starting from 2013.

[4] In 2015/16 and 2016/17, as compared to target, agricultural credit has been about 15 per cent higher.

per cent in order to avoid distress sales. In 2017/18, the Central government started interest subvention of 5 per cent per annum to farmers for short-term crop loans of up to one year, if their debt servicing was prompt.

Many farmers have to effectively pay only 4 per cent interest on loans. In case farmers do not repay the crop loans in time, they would still be eligible for interest subvention of 2 per cent. The subsidy from the Central government's budget has tripled since 2015, although it seems to have reached a plateau (see Table 12.1). During 2016/17, the outstanding quantum of short-term crop loans stood at ₹6.23 trillion, surpassing the target of ₹6.15 trillion.

Table 12.1: Interest Subvention for Providing Short-term Credit to Farmers (₹ billion)

2009/10	20.1
2014/15	60.0
2016/17	134.0
2017/18	130.5
2018/19 (BE)	150.0
2018/19 (RE)	149.9
2019/20 (BE)	180.0

Source: Union Budget documents

The Union Budget of 2014/15 put in place a scheme under which half a million Joint Liability Groups of 'Bhoomi

Heen Kisan' (landless farmers) would be financed through the National Bank for Agriculture and Rural Development, in order to augment flow of credit to landless farmers cultivating land as tenant farmers, lessees or share croppers, and small and marginal farmers as well as other poor individuals in rural areas. The experience of catalysing bank-credit flows to agriculture and expanding the panoply of subventions begs the question: are we substituting credit for other policy interventions? Indeed, this issue prompted the RBI's Expert Committee to Revise and Strengthen the Monetary Policy Framework to recommend a revisit of the need for subventions on interest rates for lending to agriculture in 2014.

Despite the sizeable volume of subsidized and directed credit flows as well as the various fiscal incentives, Indian agriculture is beset with deep-seated, well-documented distortions that render it vulnerable to high volatility. It has perennially been characterized by low investment, archaic irrigation practices, monsoon dependence, fragmentation of land holdings and low levels of technology. Lack of property rights and low initial net worth of farmers add to the constraints. Consequently, a considerable flux in output and prices is common, imposing large losses on farmers and potentially imprisoning them in a circle of indebtedness with disturbing frequency. Therefore, in the absence of coordinated and sustained efforts to put in place elements of a virtuous cycle of enhancing incomes on a long-term basis, loan waivers have periodically emerged as a quick fix to ease farmers' distress. It is unclear what the electoral implications are.

Often, *both* incumbent and challenger announce waivers in the lead-up to state elections.

A brief history of farm loan waivers in India may be in order. The first major nationwide farm loan waiver was undertaken in 1990 and the cost to the national exchequer was around ₹100 billion, which works out to ₹506 billion at today's prices using the GDP deflator. The second major waiver was under the Agricultural Debt Waiver and Debt Relief scheme of 2008 amounting to ₹520 billion (0.9 per cent of GDP) or ₹813 billion at current prices using the GDP deflator. Unlike the 1990 scheme that aimed at providing blanket relief to all farmers up to a certain loan amount, the 2008 scheme waived debt for certain classes of cultivators. In 2014, Andhra Pradesh and Telangana announced a farm loan waiver of ₹240 billion and ₹170 billion respectively (Table 12.2). Beginning with Tamil Nadu in 2016, domino effects have spread in 2017 to several states and the total cost of loan waivers announced amounts to around ₹1.3 trillion (0.8 per cent of GDP). There are two observations from the data, which are a reflection of the fiscal reality at the state level, mirroring that at the Centre, alluded to in Chapter 1:

First, states roll out the waiver over several years – it is not a one-shot delivery despite promise of prompt relief. Second, hardly any government reaches the stated aim even after three to four years.[5]

---

[5] Telangana is a notable exception; it has delivered more than the quantum of the initial announcement.

Table 12.2: Loan Waivers Since 2014 (₹ billion)

State	Year of Announce-ment	Amount Announced	2014/15	2015/16	2016/17	2017/18	2018/19	2019/20 (BE)
Andhra Pradesh	2014/15	240	40.0	7.4	35.1	36.0	8.8	
as % GSDP			0.9	0.1	0.6	0.6	0.1	
Telangana	2016/17	170	42.5	42.5	29.6	40.2		60.0
as % GSDP			1	0.9	0.6	0.7		0.9
Tamil Nadu	2017/18	52.8			16.8	18.7	8.8	8.1
as % GSDP					0.2	0.2	0.1	0.1
Maharashtra	2017/18	340.2				150.2	65.0	4.1
as % GSDP						0.8	0.3	0

State	Year of Announce-ment	Amount Announced	2014/15	2015/16	2016/17	2017/18	2018/19	2019/20 (BE)
Uttar Pradesh	2017/18	363.6				211.0	55.0	6.0
as % GSDP						2	0.5	0.1
Punjab	2018/19	100				3.5	55.0	30.0
as % GSDP						0.1	1.4	0.7
Karnataka	2018/19	440				39.2	119.7	126.5
as % GSDP						0.4	1.1	1
Rajasthan	2018/19	180					30.0	32.4
as % GSDP							0.4	0.4
Madhya Pradesh	2018/19	365					50.0	800.0
as % GSDP							0.9	1.4

State	Year of Announcement	Amount Announced	2014/15	2015/16	2016/17	2017/18	2018/19	2019/20 (BE)
Chattisgarh	2018/19	610					42.2	50.0
as % GSDP							1.8	2
Total		2,312.6	82.5	49.9	81.5	498.8	434.5	397.0
as % of state gov't total expenditure			0.40%	0.20%	0.30%	1.80%	1.20%	1.20%
as % to GDP			0.10%	0.00%	0.10%	0.30%	0.20%	0.20%
Memo: Maharashtra	December 2020	≈235 (reported)						7.5 (reported)

Agriculture Credit

The pros and cons of agricultural debt relief have been widely debated and literature has evolved around the theme. Alongside the beneficial effects in terms of clearing the debt overhang of farm households, negative side effects in the form of faulty targeting of beneficiaries and resulting discrimination, incentivizing wilful defaulters (who game the system) and erosion of credit discipline have been cited.

The other side of the debate – the implications for macroeconomic conditions and policies – can be briefly explored. The first impact of any loan waiver is on the balance sheet of lending institutions. This is inherent in the inevitable lags, the timing of impact and the arrival of compensation from the government. In the interregnum, the quality of assets deteriorates and bridge provisions crowd out new loans. In the second round, loan waivers impact the state of public finances in the form of higher than budgeted revenue expenditure. This, in turn, has to be financed by additional market borrowings, which pushes up interest rates, not just for the states but for the entire economy. A collateral damage is that private borrowers are crowded out of the finite pool of investible resources as the cost of borrowing rises. Even if the loan waiver is accommodated within budgetary provisions, it will force cutbacks in other heads of expenditure. Experience has shown that the most vulnerable category is capital expenditure. In turn, this will entail deterioration in the quality of spending and inter alia lead to adverse implications for productivity as asset-augmenting investment, including for the sector itself – for example, irrigation works, cold storage chains etc. – is foregone. If infrastructural constraints are binding, a reduction in capital expenditure for the sector that would have benefitted from this outlay could even be inflationary as costs – including time value/opportunity cost of delays and material damages – creep up as a result of physical capacity constraints becoming even more acute and attendant congestion costs/charges. If, on the other hand, budgetary provisions are exceeded, higher spending and widening of the fiscal deficit have, as experience has shown, inflationary consequences, and possible spillovers that could undermine external viability (the twin deficit argument). Also, research points to undesirable welfare effects because, ultimately, loan waivers involve a transfer of resources from taxpayers to borrowers. Consumption redistribution effects have also been reported.

It is not surprising that farm loan waivers have stirred up considerable passion and polarized opinions. While in no way detracting from the acute distress that farmers face with every disruption in crop cycles, it is important to recognize that there are externalities that spread out beyond the farm sector. Eventually, other economic agents and other parts of the economy get affected. How can this overflow be minimized? How do we defray the incidence of the burden on taxpayers? From a policy perspective, what needs to be done to move away from palliatives in the form of debt relief and towards a more durable solution that enhances welfare all around? Many elements of this optimal approach are well known – crop insurance, infrastructure, irrigation, technology-enabled productivity improvements and opening up the farm economy to market forces and open trade. The government's initiative to establish a nationwide market

Agriculture Credit

for agricultural produce, through eNAM, the Pradhan Mantri Fasal Bima Yojana, the Pradhan Mantri Krishi Sinchai Yojana, the Paramparagat Krishi Vikas Yojana and the national drive towards financial inclusion are important initiatives in this direction. The coming to fruition of these initiatives holds the potential of achieving the mission of doubling farmers' income over time. We need to ensure that their benefits percolate down to the intended recipients.

13

PREVENTIVE VIGILANCE[1]

IT IS AN ACCEPTED norm of organizing human societies that with the right to liberty comes good governance, the latter being designed around laws (formal governance) or norms (informal governance) restricting excessive exertions of the right to liberty: Where individual actions are deemed to generate harmful consequences (negative externalities) on the rest of the society,

---

[1] This chapter is an edited version of a lecture delivered at the Central Vigilance Commission, New Delhi, 20 September 2018. I would like to thank Viral Acharya and Lily Vadera for their help. The lecture was in memory of Deena Khatkhate, who served in the RBI from 1955 to 1968.

laws or norms – backed by an enforcement machinery – draw a line as to what is acceptable human behaviour. Governance could be for the society as a whole or an individual firm or entity or a group of entities (for example, the public sector). An important term that we come across, especially in the public sector, is *Vigilance*.[2]

Vigilance is defined in dictionaries as 'action or state of keeping careful watch for possible danger or difficulties'. It takes several forms, which are often classified as:

1. **Preventive vigilance**, which is aimed at reducing the occurrence of a lapse (violation of a law, a norm or, generally speaking, a governance requirement);
2. **Detective vigilance**, which is aimed at identifying and verifying the occurrence of a lapse; and finally,
3. **Punitive vigilance**, which is aimed at deterring the occurrence of a lapse.

This chapter attempts a conceptual framework, based on the economic theory of incentives, which helps understand the various aspects of vigilance, how they interact with each other and why preventive vigilance often takes centre stage in the government or public sector institutions as an essential tool of good governance.

---

2 The Central Vigilance Commission was established in 1964 by the Government of India to address corruption in the government sector.

Gary Becker's 'Crime and Punishment'[3]

The modern economic theory of corruption and how to prevent it emanates largely from Gary Becker's insightful and seminal pieces on *Crime and Punishment* during 1968–1974.[4] Gary Becker, a young economist at the University of Chicago, took the theory away from moral and ethical basis to one based on optimal human behaviour in response to the presented economic incentives. He examined his own behaviour with regard to committing parking violations when rushing to work, which involved trading off the expected cost of illegal parking in a convenient spot – which he roughly calculated as the likelihood of getting a parking ticket violation multiplied by the parking fine (assuming non-payment of the fine would be too costly not to pay up) – against the benefit in the form of convenience and reaching his class in time. Often, this calculation prompted him to opt for the parking violation, as legal parking in an inconveniently located garage did not seem economically attractive!

Becker extrapolated from his own daily behaviour an important economic insight. (As an aside, 'economics' derives

---

3 Becker, Gary S., 'Crime and Punishment: An Economic Approach', in *Journal of Political Economy,* Chicago Journals, 76(2), March–April 1968, pp. 169–217.

4 Becker, Gary S., *Essays in the Economics of Crime and Punishment.* New York: National Bureau of Economic Research, Columbia University Press, 1974.

from the Greek word 'oikonomika' (οἰκονομία), which means 'household management' and was the name of a treatise by Aristotle.) The insight was that criminals in society do the same calculation of the probability of getting caught times the potential punishment while determining whether to choose a criminal lifestyle and what crimes to engage in; conversely, if criminals responded in this manner to economic incentives rather than (only) because they had character flaws or mental illnesses, then how should laws and their enforcement be organized taking into account the costs of enforcement, and might it be excessively costly and economically undesirable in practice to reduce crime rates to zero?

Building on this fundamental insight that governance lapses may be rational choices rather than mental illnesses or character flaws in transgressors, we could consider a simple but instructive conceptual framework that may help understand how preventive, detective and punitive vigilance work with each other and should be designed given the rational best response of citizens or employees, who, given the incentives, would all be treated uniformly as potential offenders.

A Conceptual Framework

The framework is illustrated in the following schematic of how vigilance and employee actions are sequenced in a typical institutional setting. Let us walk through it step by step.

Figure 13.1: Vigilance – A Simple Model

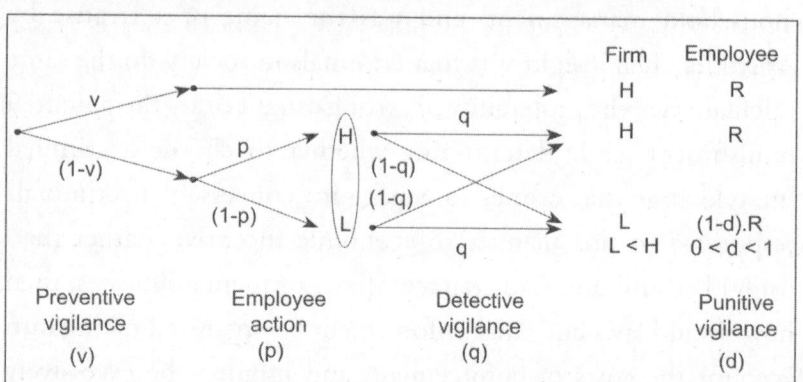

The employee is in control of an action whose outcome can be 'good' or 'bad'. If the outcome is good, the firm's cash flow or value is higher at H as compared to L, when the outcome is bad ($L < H$). The employee's *effort* is denoted as p and determines in part the likelihood that the outcome would be good (the rest being purely due to chance or background noise). The employee bears an exertion cost from undertaking this effort (so, all else equal, prefers shirking), or alternatively has some private gains (side benefits from a bad outcome for the institution). This cost creates a potential wedge between what is privately optimal for the employee and what is optimal for the institution.

Recognizing this wedge, the institution (or its regulator) puts in place preventive vigilance (v), detective vigilance (q) and punitive vigilance (d):

Preventive Vigilance

Preventive vigilance (v) reduces the likelihood of employee control over the action in the first place, that is, it puts in place safeguards such that employee lapses are less likely to occur.

Detective vigilance comes into play before the outcome has actually been realized (this is shown in the schematic as the oval box around the outcomes H and L). Its precision is denoted by q. The higher the q is, more precise is detective vigilance in identifying the good (bad) outcome indeed as the good (bad) outcome; conversely, ($1-q$) captures the error rate of detective vigilance whereby it detects the good (bad) outcome as bad (good). There are alternative ways of modelling detective vigilance. For instance, it may seek not just to identify when the outcome would have turned out to be low, but also aim to nip it in the bud so as to reverse it to a good outcome. In other words, detective vigilance in some cases may catch lapses and correct them. In yet another variant, detective vigilance could also be modelled as identifying only the low outcome possibility with some likelihood but not being able to reverse the outcome. Depending on the setting, one formulation may be more suitable than the others.

Punitive vigilance reduces the employee reward in the good-outcome scenario, denoted as R, to ($1-d$).R, in the bad-outcome scenario, where $d > 0$. The punishment $d.R$ serves an incentive for the employee to invest in increasing the good outcome likelihood. Typically, in such setups, the value of $R < H$ is pinned down based on the employee contract being attractive enough relative to reservation opportunities such as alternative job offers for employees or payoffs from remaining unemployed.

An example can help visualize the structure more concretely. Consider, for instance, procurement at a government institution. Efficient procurement would lead to a higher value for the institution by ensuring that quality is met at the cheapest cost. In order to reduce employee discretion in the procurement process, which could potentially lead to compromised choices, preventive vigilance is put in place in terms of designing the procurement process ('L1'), requiring procurement be undertaken only through, for example, an electronic tendering process, etc. Detective vigilance is also put in place in the form of a concurrent/internal audit within each department of the institution that tries to ensure that lapses are caught and fixed before they lead to the final procurement decision. Finally, in case a violation of procurement guidelines is found ex-post in spite of the other vigilance mechanisms, the central vigilance office of the institution undertakes a disciplinary action against the involved employee.

Technical assumptions

Coming back to the conceptual framework for vigilance, to derive the equilibrium solution in the setup and understand its properties, the following intuitive assumptions are made:

- Employee effort (p) leads to exertion cost that is progressively costly (increasing and sufficiently convex) so as to rule out the corner solution that perfect governance can be implemented in practice.

- Similarly, investing in preventive vigilance (v) and detective vigilance (q) becomes prohibitively expensive beyond a point, that is, the costs of increasing v and q are increasing and convex enough so as to rule out the corner solution of perfect governance.
- In a similar vein, there are limits on punishment levels: one being that there is limited liability so that employee's pecuniary reward even in the bad-outcome scenario can only be positive ($d < 1$) even if it is lower than the reward in case of the good outcome; further, there may be lower bounds on the bad-outcome reward as the institution may be constrained by (un-modelled) side-effects such as the costs of dealing with grievance redressal and legal recourse being undertaken by the employee in case the punishment for low-outcome scenario being realized is too severe.

Key 'insights'

Along the lines of Gary Becker's seminal analysis, this simple framework for understanding vigilance leads to the following insights:

1. Detective and punitive vigilance are strategic complements: the greater the punishment, the more useful it is to detect. Conversely, having a high penalty is ineffective (given concomitant side-effects or costs) when the quality of detection is poor.
2. Preventive and detective (as well as punitive) vigilance are strategic substitutes: the lower the detection and

punishment, the more useful it is to prevent lapses at the outset since detective and punitive vigilance do not provide adequate incentives. This is important and will be discussed further in the context of public sector institutions.

3. Preventive vigilance dominates other forms for dealing with lapses outside one's control: the above schematic potentially allows the analysis of how to tackle vigilance design with human effort (which is under one's control) versus human error (which is outside one's control). As an extreme case, suppose that there is no control under the employee to affect the outcomes (p is fixed). Then punishment achieves absolutely nothing in improving outcomes. In this case, preventive vigilance, which effectively reduces the chance of a lapse in the first place, dominates detective and punitive vigilance. Detective vigilance may nevertheless be effective in identifying lapses which occur due to pure chance and possibly for reversing the bad outcomes to good ones.

Dynamic considerations

Outside of the simple one-period or static model outlined above, there are dynamic considerations that may be important in the real-world design of vigilance processes.

One, it might be attractive for an institution to undertake punitive vigilance beyond what is desirable in a purely myopic sense for the purposes of setting a *precedent*; in other words, so as to deter recurrence and build a reputation or create a credible culture for zero or low tolerance for repetitive lapses.

Two, in practice, poor governance outcomes may not simply be due to optimal incentive-based behaviour, but also due to the presence of habitual offenders (an employee 'type', so to speak). In such a setting, there may be learning over time on a given employee's type that can help separate type from pure background noise; when this is the case, some weeding out may be necessary based on the initial detection phase which only after a few periods leads to a punitive vigilance outcome, as it becomes certain that employee type is above a threshold in terms of repetitive lapses that cannot be attributed over time to just chance.

The reasoning why these observations imply an essential role for preventive vigilance in good governance, especially in public sector institutions, is worth exploring.

What vigilance is likely to work best in a public sector institution?

Punitive vigilance is difficult in a public sector institution for several reasons. The rewards are low to start with, thereby limiting the possibility of downward revisions. Given this constraint, disciplinary actions that limit the chances of career progression are often the preferred punishment. However, this has the misfortune of demotivating employees beyond the point of their career when punitive vigilance action is undertaken. This could, in principle, be dealt with a 'golden handshake'; however, the insurance that public sector jobs offer is often a key attractive feature of these jobs, given the lack of significant upside financial rewards. While there are ways to fine-tune pecuniary incentives and career-based rewards for greater effectiveness even within these constraints, it is fair to conclude that their 'bite' is not as strong as in the private sector.

In turn, given the first insight (Key Insight 1) from the model, detective vigilance too is rendered somewhat ineffective. Put simply, detection does not lead to punitive outcomes (except perhaps in extreme or egregious cases and over time) so that investment in detective vigilance does not guarantee the desired reduction in incidence of lapses, even though it might help, in some cases, to arrest the slide and contain with remedial measures.

As a result, given the second insight (Key Insight 2) from the model, preventive vigilance takes centre stage and becomes a key effective tool of governance in a public sector institution. When lapses can arise due to background noise outside of the employee control (which is often the case in the public sector due to the complexity of the interaction with a multitude of other public sector entities), punitive vigilance becomes even less attractive due to further demotivation that it might induce; in turn, so does detective vigilance. In other words, while not taking away from the need to engage in some detective and punitive vigilance, preventive vigilance is conceptually likely to be the most effective governance mechanism at public sector institutions.

These observations have substantive relevance for understanding how one might tighten governance in practice, for instance, in lending outcomes – underwriting or screening, monitoring and recovering post default – at banks, a setting that is beset with many of the features highlighted in the chapter.

14

REGULATION AND POLICIES IN A WORLD OF EXCESSIVE FINANCIALIZATION[1]

TOTAL GLOBAL EXTERNAL LIABILITIES – debt and non-debt – have grown from 30 per cent to 185 per cent of

---

1 The chapter is an edited version of my intervention at the 32nd Annual G30 International Banking Seminar, 15 October 2017 at the Inter-American Development Bank, Washington, D.C. I am thankful to Bhupal Singh and Michael Patra for their help in compiling these extensive remarks. (Some data has been updated.)

global GDP between 1980 and 2018, far outpacing the growth in global trade in goods and services from 38.7 per cent to 59.4 per cent of GDP over the same period. The main vehicle of this new globalization has been cross-border banking flows, which constituted a third of international capital flows in the decade prior to the global financial crisis. In parallel, the global trade network has become increasingly interconnected through supply chains that transcend national borders, and by the advent of new players, especially from the developing world. China now accounts for about 11 per cent of the global trade and emerging market, and developing countries taken together contribute 37 per cent (up by about 15 per centage points since 2000).

During the global financial crisis, the explicit pre-crisis *assignment of policy instruments to objectives* became blurred. The experience demonstrated that macroeconomic policymaking is expected to do a fine balancing act to achieve multiple and, at times, conflicting objectives of monetary stability, fiscal stability and financial stability. Within these trade-offs, financial stability has assumed some seniority, entailing for national authorities the constant need to monitor, identify and minimize the build-up of systemic risks in financial systems and reduce spillover in the most efficient and effective way. This involves a fine dovetailing of the objectives of market efficiency into consumer protection and the management – even pre-emption – of systemic risks.

This chapter focuses on the following issues pertaining to the role of financial regulation in averting the next financial crisis:

- Globalization and adherence to global rules/standards – synergies and challenges.
- Financial regulation and suddenness of crisis incidence – regulatory intervention needs to be more anticipatory and data-based.
- Backward-looking versus forward-looking risk-based supervision – need for global systemically important banks to disclose their internal rating models.
- Too big to fail (TBTF) and moral hazard.
- Adequacy of global financial safety nets in the context of the size and speed of crises – gaps and discriminatory practices in the international financial architecture.

1. Globalization and Global Rules/Standards

Emerging market economies (EMEs) have undoubtedly benefitted from globalization, but they are also more exposed than before to vulnerabilities that come with globalization. As we access markets abroad and spread our activities on a global scale, our financial systems are also required to embrace global norms, especially on capital, risk recognition and accounting standards; monetary policy based on some rule relating to a nominal anchor such as inflation; fiscal policy based on a budget or expenditure rule; and market-based exchange rate regimes, complemented by strong and effective financial sector regulation and supervision, corporate governance and enforcement rules, and bankruptcy and resolution architecture (Patel, 2014; 2016).[2]

Markets inherently impose these exacting standards of discipline when they allow access to banks and corporates. For example, international capital tends to punish monetary and fiscal indiscipline severely. Even as some shocks tend to be impervious to fundamentals, economies with sound, prudent, transparent and accountable macro-policy frameworks have demonstrated success in containing negative externalities as well as in restoring normalcy faster. In this context, farsighted policy frameworks tie down policy actions to final goals. Some of us may think that rules are a cost imposed on us in the form of sacrifice of independence and sovereignty. While all rules may not best fit India, the ones that are highlighted below, specifically, monetary, fiscal and accounting, are widely accepted by reasonable people as a basic minimum.

First, fiscal rules are institutionalized or legally binding tenets that commit authorities to fiscal discipline. By restraining expenditure or deficits, they support overall macroeconomic policies – by keeping public debt within sustainable levels, thereby preserving/upgrading the credibility of the fiscal authority as a participant in financial markets.

---

2 'Global Integration: The Constraint of Established Fiscal, Monetary and Accounting Rules', Speech at Deloitte India Conference, Mumbai, June 2014.
Remarks in the BRICS Seminar on 'Investment Flows – Challenges, Opportunities and Road Ahead', Mumbai, October 2016.

Second, a transparent and predictable monetary policy framework is, almost by definition, rule-based.

Third, while regulation is imposed from outside, corporate governance is internal to firms and is more in the nature of self-regulation, but with safeguards that principles and rules laid down by the regulations are followed conscientiously. Nevertheless, regulation and corporate governance have to complement each other.

Fourth, with globalization, operations of large firms have become transnational, and massive cross-border movement of capital requires adoption of uniform accounting standards, such as the International Financial Reporting Standards (IFRS). When these standards are applied rigorously and consistently, investors, regulators and other stakeholders all benefit with higher quality information to make decisions.

It is imperative for banks in EMEs to adhere to standards emanating from the global standard-setting bodies. Although challenges persist in adopting standards like IFRS in EMEs, the future-oriented provisioning framework is beneficial. Banks generally tend to delay provisioning for bad loans until cyclical downturns have already set in and it is too late, possibly magnifying the impact of the economic cycle on banks' income and capital. In such circumstances, providing for and recognizing actual and potential loan losses at an earlier stage in the credit cycle could potentially mitigate procyclicality, and foster financial stability.

2. Financial Regulation and Suddenness of Crisis Incidence: Need for Regulatory Intervention to Be More Anticipatory and Data-based[3]

In the context of financial stability, acceptable regulation should have three broad characteristics: first, regulation ought to be predictable. A regulation susceptible to forbearing instincts carries the concomitant chance of risk-inducing behaviour by stakeholders. Secondly, regulation should aim to shoehorn internal governance mechanisms of the regulated entities in an incentive-compatible way. Finally, it should aim to address information asymmetry between the key stakeholders since the lack of information often leads to herd behaviour, thus precipitating crises.

Backward-looking regulation attempts to address gaps in regulation in one sector, region and nation; but given the complexity and inter-connectedness of the financial system, activity swiftly shifts to another sector, region or nation and builds financial excesses. However, the next threat to financial stability may come from quarters that regulators are completely unaware of. Thus, forward-looking regulations are not a luxury, or, a case of excess standards, required to deal with such unforeseen risks. With the advent of big data analytics, cloud computing and artificial intelligence, we are at a stage where data can be used to model future events with certain confidence intervals, and our

---

3 Some of these points were made by me in a series of op-eds: 'Wall Street has to be pushed further', *Business Standard*, 18 August 2008. 'Yet another "master of finance"', *Business Standard*, 27 September 2008.

regulations can potentially be structured to deal with such events. The thrust on two areas – cyber security and FinTech – is a case in point. A decade back, few bankers or policymakers talked about this threat. Today these are identified as major risks to the financial system.

The allergy to intrusive regulation pre-crisis has been overturned into a necessity in the post-crisis period across advanced economies (AEs) and EMEs. In the post-crisis hyper-active regulatory environment, it is possible to develop detailed dos and don'ts to potentially avert a crisis. In such a milieu, certain basic characteristics of a regulatory framework, coupled with a supervisory regime that is responsive to investors' and other stakeholders' concerns, has the best chance of inducing prudential behaviour among regulatees. Regulators have been slapping record fines on major banks and financial institutions for making undue profits or masking their problems by fraudulently rigging rates. A lot of mis-selling of products by banks in certain jurisdictions has also raised serious concerns among regulators, which is attracting more observance-heavy regulation with a bearing on banks' compliance costs.

3. Reliance on Internal Rating-Based Risk Assessment by Global Banks: Black Box Requires Reasonable Disclosure and Transparency[4]

The last financial crisis has prompted doubts that the internal ratings-based approach may have been used opportunistically to

---

[4] I had first made this argument in: 'Banking: Time for the Full Monty!', *Economic Times*, 11 February 2008.

minimize capital requirements, thus helping banks to disguise credit bubbles by keeping their risk-weighted assets artificially low. The evidence suggests that internal risk estimates employed for regulatory purposes systematically under-predict actual default rates. Supervisory confidence in risk weights is critical to the success of the regulatory framework. Work of the Basel Committee on Banking Supervision on the implementation of the Basel capital framework has gathered evidence that significant variations in capital outcomes generated by internal models (with respect to portfolios with similar risk profiles) may be unwarranted. Thus, there is a need to improve transparency and comparability across internal models to ensure that internal ratings are built and validated on the basis of a set of common standards. A reasonable degree of transparency and disclosure will help establish the credibility of the risk assessment models being used by many large global banks. As the saying goes, 'Sunlight is said to be the best disinfectant.'

4. Too Big to Fail and Moral Hazard

There are concerns related to the implicit government guarantee for TBTF institutions. These concerns derive from the belief that the TBTF status gives large banks a competitive edge and incentives to take on additional risks. If investors believe that the largest banks are too big to fail, they will be willing to offer them funding at a discount. Together with expectations of rescues, this discount gives the TBTF banks incentives to engage in riskier activities. This, in turn, could drive smaller banks that compete with them to take on further risks, spiralling the hazards of the entire financial system.

Regulatory labelling of systemically important financial institutions/systemically important banks (SIFIs/SIBs) may convey the promise of implicit taxpayer-sponsored bailouts for uninsured deposits in case of insolvency. While they also bring in additional regulatory capital prescriptions to act as a loss absorbent, in a competitive capital market, the possibility of SIFIs/SIBs taking additional risks to earn the additional returns on capital and thereby negating the role of additional capital can never be ruled out. Hence, the nature of supervisory oversight of SIFIs/SIBs ought to be a lot more *intrusive* relative to other financial institutions. The bank bailouts experience in Europe underscored that the political economy around this is more important than regulatory labelling.

5. Inadequacy of Global Financial Safety Nets and Discriminatory Central Bank Swap Lines Force EMEs to Self-insurance

Monetary policy stances of systemic Central banks, geo-political developments and uncertainty surrounding the direction of macroeconomic policies in AEs have been the main push factors driving the influx of capital flows to EMEs. For these recipient economies, this has translated into heightened financial market volatility with some harmful implications for their growth prospects and for macroeconomic and financial stability. By and large, EMEs have absorbed the shocks by maintaining fairly open capital accounts and by strengthening their macro fundamentals through prudent policies. Yet, as high intensity events starting with the taper tantrum in 2013 have shown, macroeconomic fundamentals do not matter in the face of these large and sudden movements of capital, and their economies remain vulnerable to rapid materialization of risks.

So far, our quest for a robust, equitable and quickly deployable global financial safety net (GFSN) has remained elusive. As a consequence, EMEs have had to buffer themselves by maintaining reserves and managing financial volatility through a combination of policy instruments, including a macro-prudential/capital flow management (CFM) toolkit, which are essentially pre-emptive in nature. Given the stigma attached to IMF facilities and their quest for *self-insurance*, EMEs have resorted to building foreign exchange reserves as the 'first line of defence' to calm volatility in financial markets and to provide adequate liquidity buffers for sudden stop and reversals. Additionally, regional financial safety nets have emerged to complement the agenda of financial stability.

In the post global financial crisis era, the GFSN has grown significantly with large accumulation of reserves by countries, and increase in various bilateral and multilateral swap arrangements. Global reserves grew from US$2 trillion in 2000 to US$13 trillion by the end of 2018, 57 per cent of which are held by EMEs. However, according to the fund's Assessing Reserves Adequacy metric, a fair number of EMEs (especially in Eastern Europe and Latin America) fall short of the range of 100–150 per cent of the composite metrics that are considered adequate for precautionary purposes. Bilateral swap lines between Central banks expanded dramatically during the crisis and have further increased since then. The bilateral swaps are dominated by China's extensive network of renminbi swap lines – thirty-three swap lines in place in 2017 valued at US$460 billion. BRICS countries have established a US$100 billion multi-country currency swap arrangement aiming to provide short-term liquidity for members and to address balance of payments difficulties. Other regional financing arrangements that have emerged are the Eurasian Fund for Stabilization and Development with contributions of US$8.5 billion, the Arab Monetary Fund and the Latin American Reserve Fund.

With every new tail event, however, the churn becomes larger, the volatility ever higher, threatening to overwhelm the modest defences that EMEs are able to muster. It is in this context that attention has to be drawn to the stark asymmetry prevailing in the provision of swap lines by systemic central banks. In fact, it is not an exaggeration to describe the present situation as *virtual apartheid*, by which systemic Central banks protect themselves and their self-interest. Meanwhile, EMEs that are at the receiving end of global financial turbulence are denied access. The time has come to end this sectarian approach and make available the access to swap lines. While EMEs have shown a degree of resilience to the turbulence over the last decade and a half, they are vulnerable to liquidity and bridge financing gaps that are transitory but debilitating. Access to swap lines will assist them in managing these risks better and help prevent hazards from assuming systemic proportions, thereby threatening global financial stability. We must learn from the lessons of the global financial crisis and act expeditiously and comprehensively to establish a broader swap network. In its absence, the macroeconomic environment of each country will inform the choice of policy instruments. In such a milieu, there cannot be any common code or uniform approach to capital account liberalization.

There has been considerable focus, possibly with increasing impetus, on macro-prudential measures (MPMs). However, while legitimacy of MPMs has been well established, the same legitimacy for CFMs has not been universally accepted despite an explicit endorsement by the IMF for selective use of CFMs. It is important to recognize that amid global financial cycles and the inexorability of the trilemma, corner solutions are not feasible. So, soft capital account management becomes a necessity – keeping external debt within practicable limits and prudence regarding the external sector help strengthen financial and macroeconomic stability.

The challenge before us is to identify what is going to strike us next. Hence, any regulation of the financial system should take a pre-emptive approach and consider the potential fragility of banks alongside all other elements of the financial system. This would prevent regulatory arbitrage and help to ex ante determine supervisory guiderails, that is, rules of the game, for the system.

15

REMARKS AT THE MEGHNAD DESAI ACADEMY OF ECONOMICS[1]

Role of Economists and Researchers in Shaping Policy

THE VITAL ROLE OF economists in shaping public perceptions and discourses and in designing strategic policies in the

---

1 The remarks have been edited and considerably shortened compared to the original. I am thankful to Bhupal Singh for his help.

corporate sector, Central banks, governments and multilateral institutions, is more often than not unsung. Rigorous research and training helps in formulating informed set of policy choices and consequent decisions. In the domain of public policy, we have to distinguish between the direct and the indirect impact that economists can make. The former is what we usually think of when we consider how experts might affect formulation of a policy, say, minimizing the subsidy burden on the exchequer. However, their substantive contribution to policymaking may take place through less direct routes such as through their research by provoking policymakers to think about economic problems and challenges in different ways compared to the past.

Policymakers, too, have a crucial role in creating an enabling environment for economists to contribute to society. In this context, the Government of India has to be lauded for instituting landmark reforms in the areas of monetary policy and fiscal federalism. One cannot and should not underestimate the sagacity and uncommon courage of the government in undertaking reforms that can only be described as truly transformative. These will shape, for the better, our economic evolution in the years and decades to come.

In 2016, the government legislated amendments to the RBI Act to invest the Reserve Bank of India with the specific mandate to operate the monetary policy framework of the country whose primary objective is to 'maintain price stability while keeping in mind the objective of growth'. This was a fundamental shift in the institutional architecture for the conduct of monetary policy, with the formal transition to a flexible inflation targeting framework and the relinquishing of the monetary policy decision by the RBI governor to a six-member monetary policy committee. Another momentous reform is the establishment of the goods and services tax council whereby the Government of India has created an effective institutional mechanism for cooperative federalism. Along with the state governments, it has offered a refreshing counter-narrative to the divisive course of the international federal dialogue, voluntarily choosing to relinquish and then pool sovereignty for a larger collective cause. These steps are unprecedented in the history of our nation in that they show the government's commitment to sound public policy by establishing institutions and ceding power to them to perform functions vital for securing and entrenching macroeconomic and financial stability.

Economists are often misunderstood and at times maligned. To illustrate, economists are heaped with the criticism that they failed to see and predict the 2007/08 global financial crisis, and this has dented the credence of their profession. To my mind this may not be entirely warranted, maybe even unfair. Doctors understand diseases but cannot predict when one will fall ill. The fundamental mission of economists is not that of forecasting crises but to explain how economic actors behave in the ordinary business of life and in doing so they do warn of crisis *formations*, suggest pre-emptive strategies and formulate mitigating policies that address those crises that slip through macroeconomic surveillance. More often than not, they meet with resistance. Hyman Minsky laboured in relative obscurity from the start of his academic career in the 1950s until 1996, when he died. His research about financial crises and their causes attracted little mainstream attention back then.[2] It was only in 2007 when the US subprime-mortgage crisis erupted that everyone started turning to his writings as they tried to make sense of the chaos engulfing global financial markets. The abrupt metamorphosis of a financial crisis from a state of dormancy or calm is now often referred to as the 'Minsky' moment. In another striking example, George Akerlof's landmark paper 'The Market for Lemons'[3] was rejected by several journals before it was finally published. As time passed, his seminal paper brought home the wisdom that adverse selection was a fundamental cause of market failures and the idea turned into a foundation stone of information economics. New and fresh ideas often meet a wall of resistance as they tend to challenge inertia in the existing shores of thinking.

For the Central banking profession, thinking new and fresh is demanded by the ever-changing world in which we operate. To give an example, the RBI has been striving to understand household and firm behaviour through its surveys and the associated analysis. However, the need now is to understand micro-level price formation dynamics in new dimensions such as e-commerce, digital transactions and big cross-sectional data. This applies to domains such as banking, non-banking financial intermediation, payments, currency management and financial

---

2 Hyman Minsky, *Stabilizing an Unstable Economy*, McGraw-Hill Professional, New York, 1986.

3 George Akerlof, 'The Market for Lemons: Quality Uncertainty and the Market Mechanism', *Quarterly Journal of Economics*, Vol. 84, 1970, pp. 488–500.

Remarks at the Meghnad Desai Academy of Economics

inclusion as well. In the absence of this type of research, policy choices could yield sub-optimal outcomes at times. There is an acute information deficit regarding the unorganized sector in India, despite its significant role in income and employment generation. The absence of official statistics has not, however, prevented economists from conducting survey-based research to help understand the dynamics.

To conclude, it may be apposite to quote Paul Romer, a pioneer of endogenous growth theory, from his much-cited paper 'The Trouble with Macroeconomics':[4]

> Even when it works well, science is not perfect... Scientists commit to the pursuit of truth even though they realise that absolute truth is never revealed. All they can hope for is a consensus that establishes the truth of an assertion in the same loose sense that the stock market establishes the value of a firm. It can go astray, perhaps for long stretches of time. But eventually, it is yanked back to reality by *insurgents* (my emphasis) who are free to challenge the consensus and supporters of the consensus who still think that getting the facts right matters.

---

4 Paul Romer, 'The Trouble with Macroeconomics', *The Commons Memorial Lecture of the Omicron Delta Epsilon Society*, 5 January 2016.

16

CONCLUSIONS AND THE TRILEMMA

IT IS APPARENT THAT the temptation to deploy GBs for catalysing aggregate demand has intensified. The culmination is a vicious cycle: as the government's headroom for running higher fiscal deficits is exhausted, GBs are encouraged to (over) lend to pump-prime the economy and boost preferred sectors. Almost inevitably, this leads to higher NPAs over time, which requires equity infusion from the government, and this eventually adds to the fiscal deficit and sovereign liabilities (for example, on account of recap bonds) in due course, anyway. The size of governments' (both Central and state) credit enhancement and guarantee obligations have also increased.

Conclusions and the Trilemma

The broad conclusion that has been universally accepted is that enterprises in India have over and over again received excessive credit during loan growth cycles, which is followed soon after with repayment problems. Rather than resolving stressed credit problems swiftly, banks – either through loan-level fudges or refusal to recognize the true asset quality of the credits – have allowed promoters in charge of enterprises to have a soft landing; this has comprised of even more bank lending so as to keep the accounts artificially in full repayment on past dues, protracted control for promoters over failed assets, and effectively granting them the ability to divert cash and assets, often outside of our jurisdictional reach.

Speedy and time-bound resolution, even liquidation, can help boost growth as it will inhibit the atrophy of capital stock that comes about from the emergence and prolongation of zombie firms and sectors.[1] Going forward, there are two potential significant drivers of bad debts, viz., the extant broad economic slowdown (even prior to COVID-19), which the RBI's stress scenario in the Financial Stability Report for June 2019 made amply clear; and the low interest coverage ratio of a fair number of highly leveraged large corporations that continue to face elevated hazard.

---

1 It is known that idleness leads to a downgrade of industrial assets. For example, the gas-based thermal plant in Ratnagiri had its 'boiler-plate' capacity reduced by about 200MW – almost 10 per cent – while a resolution was being worked out over many years for the greenfield asset.

In 2013, banks had not yet grasped the reality, the previous government was on its last legs and the regulator may not have fully appreciated the scale and urgency of the issues because of, inter alia, an incomplete sector picture. After 2014, a coherent policy scaffolding for meeting the NPA challenge has been constructed over the last five years, even as: (i) the process for executing the IBC has thrown up a worrying number of exceptions; (ii) an asset quality review for NBFCs, as also borrower categories like MSMEs, seems to have been postponed, which adds to the risk premium for the sector; and (iii) a two-tier structure of regulation could (explicitly) emerge, one for GBs and one for PBs, when the next policy boost to credit is deemed desirable.

Regulatory forbearance has played a complementary role to help matters along in this regard. Stakeholders' conducts over the years have contributed to the widespread, and justified, belief that climb-downs can be inevitably brought about. When banks are overused as tactical assets for macroeconomic management, there is a dangerous *cognitive capture*[2] of policymaking space by bankers, even in areas outside their remit.

As recently as August 2019, the Large Exposure Framework was relaxed after coming into effect only months earlier in April. In February 2020, 'living dead' borrowers in the commercial real-estate sector – under a familiar guise ('a ghost from the past', if you will) viz., ad hoc 'restructuring' – have been given a lifeline.[3]

---

2   The first time I came across this term was in the writings of Willem Buiter in the aftermath of the 2008 North Atlantic financial crisis.

3   https://www.rbi.org.in/Scripts/NotificationUser.aspx?Id=11806&Mode=0

It is estimated that over one-third of loans to builders are under moratorium.[4][5] Why not other sectors? So, again banks' published balance sheets don't convey an authentic picture, with resultant confusion.

The sovereign and the regulator face a *trilemma*: It is clear that it is not possible to: (i) have dominance of GBs in the banking sector; (ii) retain independent regulation; and (iii) adhere to public debt-GDP targets. All three are not feasible on a durable basis; only two out of three can be sustained.

If we want both a large state-sponsored presence in banking and budgetary prudence from the government, then after fiscal dominance over monetary policy, are we looking at fiscal dominance over banking regulation?

The decline in share of GBs in the banking sector should not be resisted, otherwise the cul-de-sac will be accentuated. Current trends broadly suggest that the banking sector is increasingly privatized, by stealth, much like the telecom sector has been since the early 2000s. In a manner the invisible hand is working; the cost of risk capital for GBs from the markets is too high, hence their enduring reliance on the government. Therefore, the Indian taxpayer has to decide how much of her government's revenues are earmarked to infuse capital into GBs – this will determine the latter's capabilities in the banking sphere. Government, on

---

4 Therefore, the extant relatively low NPA figure for this class of borrowers is likely to be an underestimate.

5 See 'India Financial Sector, 3Q20: Bank slippages rise; NBFC spreads start to moderate', Credit Suisse, 17 February 2020.

behalf of the taxpayer, has to assess whether return on its equity investment in GBs is value for money, since its shareholding in GBs continues to increase. Ditto for LIC life-policy holders.

Important reforms are held up against the touchstone of implications for GBs and the government. Deadlines for much-needed housekeeping regulations such as Ind AS/IFRS accounting standards, timely recognition of losses on holding of government securities, and a Basel III requirement/commitment for setting aside a capital conservation buffer – the latter postponed at the same time as the prompt corrective action parameters were ignored – have been delayed. Developments in the sector since 2018 underscore the importance of the passage of the Financial Resolution and Deposit Insurance bill to deal with failing institutions. Bringing financial service providers under the Insolvency and Bankruptcy Code is an expedient alternative. It is also a risk to the standing of the bankruptcy code, because if a financial service provider (FSP) resolution turns messy, it will undermine the credibility of the code. Foisting failing FSPs onto the IBC makes for a poor choice at many levels;[6] the proximate 'macro' one is that the IBC is designed for value maximization of failed *businesses*, not for *financial stability*. *Failing* financial institutions require a distinct streamlined resolution authority

---

6 These are known, and relate to, agency and incentive compatibility tensions that are intrinsic under the NCLT umbrella amongst economic actors, say, between NBFCs and banks, who dominate the committee of creditors.

that speedily executes a legislated playbook, which has been the international best practice post-global financial crisis.[7]

The allure to go 'back to the past' should be eschewed if we want safer banks. Undoubtedly, some reversals around regulation and execution of the IBC have occurred, which underscores that it is fragile. While there may be grounds for remaining warily optimistic, in the sense that we will not completely reset the clock to pre-2014 despite setbacks in 2019 and early 2020, we have to be vigilant that U-turns don't usher a serial bout of ever-greening and zombie borrowers; otherwise, victory over crony capitalism will, at best, be short-lived, and that the limited progress so far could turn out to be a false dawn.

Knowledgeable observers are not sanguine that we may yet squander the gains:

> 'You are encouraging bad behavior by supporting it [regulatory forbearance] and demoralising the ones with good behavior; this is akin to farm loan waiver that leads to bad credit behavior. This is nothing but kicking the can down the road, this should not be encouraged'. – Partner, PriceWaterhouse Coopers, quoted in *Economic Times*, 26 February 2020.

> 'But neither stalled projects nor the NPA crisis received speedy attention for resolution from the government, and

---

[7] All these points are drawn directly from the excellent article by Pratik Datta and Varun Marwah, 'Does IBC Work for Financial Firms?', *Business Standard*, 26 December 2020.

its sheer inability to attempt banking reforms means future crises will be hard to prevent' (Mehra, 2019).[8]
'So it is likely that India will continue to have an unhealthy banking sector. It will serve the economy poorly, make the RBI ineffective, and give the government a well-deserved bad name'. – Ashok V. Desai, *The Telegraph*, 9 September 2019.

Will episodic concerns for stability recur? The likelihood increases if there is foot dragging or, ominously, further backsliding, and the associated delays explicated in the middle chapters of the book. There has been a gradual but effective connecting of dots in the public mindspace on NPAs and the welfare of depositors. Direct stakeholders, in particular savers, have to be vigilant against risks emanating from (potential) creeping regulatory and policy complacency. Shortcuts or, worse, sweeping problems under the carpet is unlikely to work; it will only delay the unlocking of capital, hold back growth and come in the way of financing future investment efficiently. That is where we began in the initial chapters.

It is an open issue whether centralized government control alone can be effective in designing and implementing governance of banking franchise comprising around 60 per cent of the sector's deposits and assets. It would be better instead to restore regulatory and market discipline, but it is impossible to tie the hands of the

---

8 Puja Mehra, *The Lost Decade: 2008–2018*, Ebury Press, Penguin Random House India, 2019.

sovereign; pesky legislation can be easily modified or repealed and constitutional amendments are not insurmountable. Why should Indian governments do anything differently? Where is the fun in owning banks if control over operations, managing them and determining their regulation is not possible? The likelihood that *meaningful* privatization of banks will be pursued by any government is small. As the fiscal elbow room in relation to ambitious expenditure programmes narrows, governments will hold on to GBs to keep alive the 'option value' of using them for direct stimulus during economic slowdowns. The only other free lunch (for a while) is opening the spigot to short-term external inflows of all sizes and shapes.

In playwriting there is a conception known as 'Chekhov's gun': if there is a rifle hanging above the mantelpiece in Act One, it is going to be fired at someone by the end of Act Five. In the regulatory, enforcement and legal landscape around loan recoveries in India over the last three decades, the unused rifle usually disappears by Act Three, hence not credible since all stakeholders know about the preordained vanishing act. Investment in policy and regulatory integrity requires staying the course; there is no other way.

D: APPENDICES

Appendix 1

AGGRAVATED MORAL HAZARD IN THE INDIAN FINANCIAL SYSTEM[1]

ARE THE TWO SETS of events – the economic slowdown and at least the perception of an incipient (systemic) crisis in the financial sector – correlated? Several conventional reasons have been ascribed to the ongoing deceleration in India's growth and the virtually flat private sector investment, with overall investment less than 28 per cent of GDP. These are more the effects of underlying

---

1 I am thankful to the Stanford King Center on Global Development (previously Stanford Center for International Development) for permission to reproduce material from: Urjit Patel and Saugata Bhattacharya, 'The Financial Leverage Coefficient: Macroeconomic Implications of Government Involvement in Intermediation', SCID Working Paper no. 157, October 2002.

malaises. There have undoubtedly been exogenous contributors to the slowdown, including, inter alia, trade conflicts ('when elephants fight, the grass suffers'), and a global slowdown, albeit modest. It is more likely that the current disclosures of problems of a number of financial intermediaries have underlined the close links between economic growth and the financial sector. There is still, moreover, incomplete and inadequate understanding of the propagation mechanism for the shocks, despite the importance attached by policymakers to maintaining a sound financial system. The links are even more complicated if feedback mechanisms for financial sector solvency and economic activity are incorporated.

The government-owned function in the sector remains sizeable. The persisting management control of a large section of financial intermediaries (banks and non-banks) by the government has moreover been reinforced, especially over the last few years, by the increasing use of a variety of practices (payments by Central and state government agencies for procurement of infrastructure services, viz., roads, conventional electricity supply, energy from renewable sources in the private sector, etc.), that intensifies the density (direct and indirect) of government participation in this area. A prominent reason is an attempt by the government to boost public investment, partially to counter low private investment.

In this scenario, the normal mechanisms that mitigate moral hazard in agency situations are greatly weakened (see Figure A1.1).

A Model of an Endogenously Switching Financial Leverage Coefficient

It is useful to formally delineate aspects of the transmission channels that impact economic growth discussed above. The analytical scaffolding integrates diverse strands of macroeconomic

Aggravated Moral Hazard in the Indian Financial System

Figure A1.1: Schematic Diagram of Transmission Mechanism

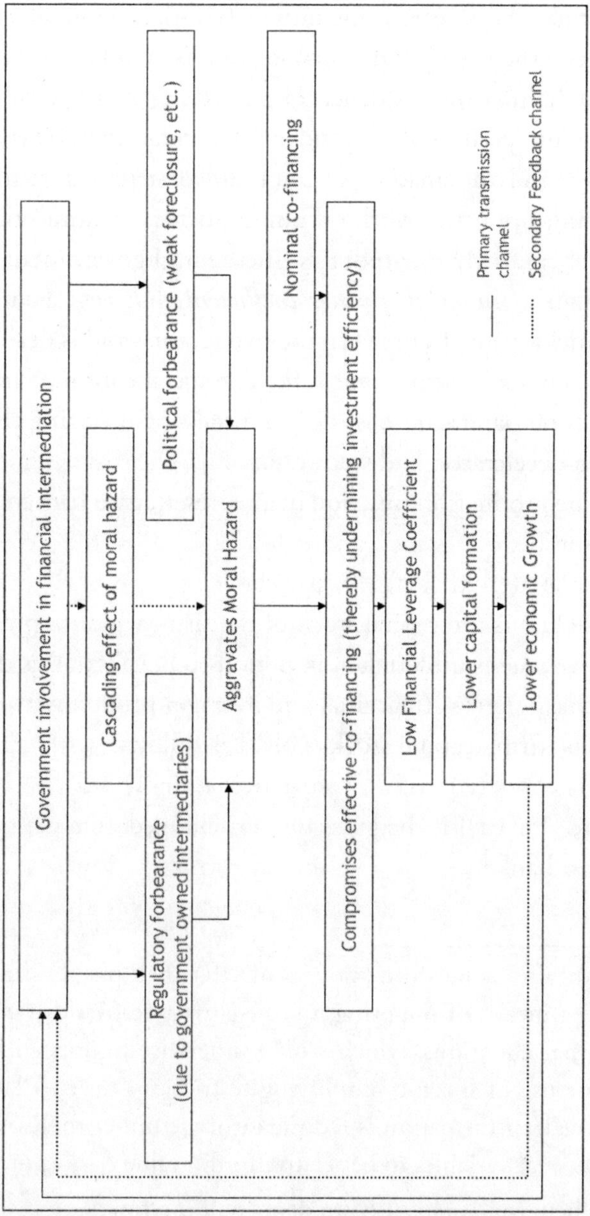

——— Primary transmission channel
········· Secondary Feedback channel

and financial research, including the financial accelerator as a link between the real and financial sectors (Bernanke and Gertler, 1999); research into the sequence of increasing fragility of the banking sector under imperfect prudential regulation (Dekle and Kletzer, 2001); and the analysis of unobserved structural 'turning points', drawing upon the work of, among others, Hamilton (1989). The model explicitly incorporates (increasing) government involvement through a *financial leverage coefficient* that acts as a transmission channel for shocks between the two sectors, and is derived within an endogenous growth framework. The specification of an endogenous structural parameter has the potential of converting the accelerator into a decelerator, and vice versa.

The production function of a representative firm in the economy is given by:

$$y(t) = \varphi(\alpha(t)) k(t), \quad \varphi' > 0, \quad \varphi'' \leq 0 \qquad (1)$$

where $k(t)$ is the capital stock of the firm, which is predetermined by investment undertaken in period $(t-1)$. $\varphi'(\alpha(t))$ is the (stochastic) gross (marginal and average) productivity of capital.[2]

The firm's capital stock evolves as follows:

$$k(t+1) = \varphi(\alpha(t)) k(t) - (1 + r(t))\iota(t) + \iota(t+1) \qquad (2)$$

where $\{1 + r(t)\}$ is the gross interest charged on a period t loan, $\iota(t)$, from a bank.[3]

---

[2] An affine transformation φ of $\alpha(t)$ in Eqn. (1) can be deployed as a means of imposing non-negativity restrictions on some of the other equations, which would otherwise have been violated upon the use of specific simplifying restrictions on $\alpha(t)$ later. Note that this transformation is redundant if we understood the values of all the real variables to be relative to the value of output, $y(t)$.

[3] The term *bank* is used to denote all intermediaries.

Let $z(t) = [k(t) - \iota(t)] / k(t)$ (3)

be the (notional) co-financing requirement. $(k-\iota)$ ($\equiv s$) is, therefore, the shareholder equity in the firm (Dekle and Kletzer, 2001).[4] With $1 \geq z \geq 0$, and the analytically simplifying assumption that shareholder consumption is zero, the lending decision rule of the bank, i.e., the maximum incremental loan amount, is given by:

$\iota(t+1) - \iota(t) = (1/z(t)) [(\varphi(\alpha(t)) - 1)k(t) - r(t)\iota(t)]$ (4)

where the term inside the square parentheses on the right side in Eqn. (4) above is the net income for the firm. Since $z(t)$ is the proportion of total capital required to be provided as equity by the firm for every unit of loan provided by the bank in each period, Eqn. (4) above says that the incremental lending by the bank, $[\iota(t+1) - \iota(t)]$, will be z per cent of $[(\varphi(\alpha(t)) - 1)k(t) - r(t)\iota(t)]$, which is the maximum investible resource of the firm. $\{z\iota(t+1)\}$ equals the gross output of the firm in period t minus the gross interest on its debt in period t, since $\iota = (1-z)k$ from the definition of z.

Combining Eqns. (2) and (4), and using Eqn. (3), the expression determining the firm's increase in capital stock is as follows:

$k(t+1) - k(t) = [(1+z(t))/z(t)][(\varphi(\alpha(t)) - 1)k(t) - r(t)\iota(t)]$ (5)

where $[(1 + z(t)) / z(t)]$ ($\equiv \omega(t)$) is a financial accelerator (FA).[5]

In the model, this accelerator is modified, with a probabilistic augmentation to account for government involvement, and becomes time-dependent. The divergence from the existing framework arises from the introduction of a distinction between the *effective* and

---

4 An interior solution for z is derived in Bernanke and Gertler (1989), with a range of projects that are mean-preserving spreads/shrinks of each other.

5 See Bernanke, Gertler and Gilchrist (1999).

notional co-financing requirements. The difference comes about from specific features that arise out of significant government involvement in financial intermediation, leading to a weakening of the profit-maximizing motive for many institutions in the sector, which is then aggravated by a lack of exit opportunities for both intermediaries and the firms that they lend to.

The concept of the effective co-financing requirement, $z^*(t)$, can be introduced.

Definition 1: Define μ as the *effective co-financing factor*.

The parameter μ is meant to differentiate the notional from the effective co-financing requirement.

Definition 2: Define the *effective co-financing parameter*, $z^*(t)$, as follows:

$$z^*(t) = [k(t) - \mu(t)\iota(t)] / k(t) \quad ; \quad \mu \geq 1 \qquad (6)$$

μ(t) in Eqn. (6) above is a formal representation of a distortion of the nominal loan component given by the bank. Our restriction on μ implies that the 'effective' loan is larger than the nominal credit facility.[6]

The effective co-financing requirement from firms against the backdrop of greater public ownership of intermediaries is less than the notional co-financing requirement under profit-maximizing behaviour when these are privately owned. Under full private ownership of all intermediaries, the notional and effective co-financing requirements should be identical (i.e., the full profit-maximizing one). Therefore, μ, with no government involvement in intermediation should be equal to one.

---

6 The effective loan may be larger than the nominal loan amount if the nominal amount, for instance, is sanctioned at a rate of interest lower than the one commensurate with the associated level of risk.

Lemma: $z^*(t) \leq z(t)$ for all $k(t)$ and $\iota(t)$.

Proof: see Proofs at the end of the Appendix (the proof, in fact, is obvious, given the definition of $z^*(t)$ in Eqn. (6) above and the restriction on $\mu(t)$).

Let μ be represented as follows:
$$\mu(t) = \theta^{\gamma(t)} ; 0 \leq \gamma \leq 1^{7}, \theta > 1 \qquad (7)$$

$\mu(t)$ is modelled as a function of two parameters, θ and $\gamma(t)$, and the latter is time varying. γ represents the '*density*' of government involvement in the financial sector and is assumed to be an (endogenous) driver of the dynamics of the model. Note that the 'density' of involvement is a broader concept than ownership: although government ownership of banks may be formally decreasing, its *involvement* may actually be on the rise.

θ is a measure of the *aggravated moral hazard* (AMH) [8] that arises due to the involvement of government in intermediation and the consequent failure of banks to institute appropriate risk-mitigation

---

7 The lower bound, strictly speaking, should be an arbitrarily small number, which avoids issues of discontinuities as $\gamma \to 0$, and is congruent with the continued involvement of government in intermediation, even in cases where the financial sector is dominated by private players.

8 The term *aggravated* has been made distinct from *enhanced*, considering the former as a parametric shift of the underlying variables as opposed to a functional dependence in the case of the latter. More explicitly, increasing moral hazard buttresses the incentives of banks to accumulate riskier portfolios, whereas an aggravated moral hazard results in a failure to initiate corrective steps to mitigate the increased hazard, for example, by increasing requirements of capital, proper risk weighting, project monitoring, etc.

measures. θ is greater than one, which is a corollary of the contention that the effective co-financing requirement for borrowers is lower than the notional co-financing requirement.

As $\gamma \to 0$, $\mu \to 1$, i.e., the effective and notional co-financing requirements converge. This is the case where 'pure' moral hazard dominates. This feature would make previous moral hazard models a nested one of the effective co-financing model.

As $\gamma \to 1$, $\mu \to \theta$, which is greater than 1, making the effective co-financing requirement less than the notional. As γ increases to 1, the co-financing required decreases more than proportionately.

Using Eqns. (6) and (7),
$$z^*(t) = [k(t) - \theta^{\gamma(t)} \iota(t)] / k(t) = \{[k(t) - \iota(t)] / k(t)\} - \{(\theta^{\gamma(t)} - 1) \iota(t) / k(t)\} = z(t) - \beta(t) \tag{8}$$
where $\beta(t) \equiv z^*(t) - z(t) = (\theta^{\gamma(t)} - 1) \iota(t) / k(t)$. Figure A1.2 below is a depiction of a representative divergence of the effective co-financing requirement from nominal one, as government involvement in the financial sector increases. $\beta(t)$ is 0 when $\gamma \to 0$ and increases to θ' ($< \theta$) as $\gamma \to 1$.

Figure A1.2: Characteristics of (z – z*) as a Function of γ

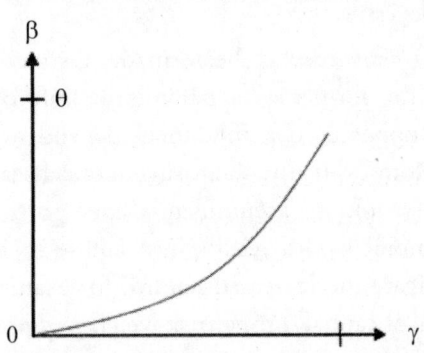

$z^*(t)$, the effective co-financing requirement, is the basis of a financial leverage coefficient.[9]

Definition 3: Define $\omega^*(t)$ as the financial leverage coefficient (FLC); formally:

$$\omega^*(t) = (1+z^*(t))/z^*(t) \qquad (9)$$

Substituting for $z^*(t)$, and with a little manipulation,

$$\omega^*(t) = 1 + [z(t)+ \{(1 - \mu(t))\,(\iota(t)\,/\,k(t))\}]^{(-1)} \qquad (10)$$

Proposition: There exists a value of $\mu(t)$, M, such that $\omega^*(t) < 0$ for all $\mu(t) > M$ and $\omega^*(t) > 0$ for all $\mu(t) < M$. Given suitable restrictions on θ, this value is unique.

Corollary: Given θ, there exists a value of $\gamma(t)$, Γ, such that $\omega^*(t) < 0$ for all $\gamma(t) > \Gamma$ and $\omega^*(t) > 0$ for all $\gamma(t) < \Gamma$.

Proof: See end of this Appendix.

Depending on the actual value of $\mu(t)$, the absolute value of the term in square brackets might become greater than one, and $\omega^*(t)$ then becomes negative (see Figure A1.3 below). Denote Γ as this threshold level of the density of government involvement in intermediaries, on reaching which a regime change is triggered in the co-financing requirement, and consequently in the FLC. Formally, Γ is defined such that $\omega^*(t) = 0$.

---

9 A microeconomic foundation of this is that government-owned financial intermediaries both lend to firms as well as invest in them. Even had these intermediaries not invested, the fact that they are less commercially oriented than private intermediaries also augments the financial decelerator, disregarding, for instance, sub-optimal debt-equity ratios compared to industry standards and norms.

Figure A1.3: A Representative Characterization of ω* as a Function of γ

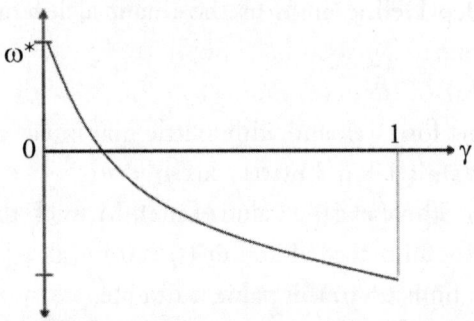

ω*(t) is a generalization of the FA, which, as noted earlier, was introduced to explain the amplification of adverse real shocks in the economy, arising endogenously from credit-market frictions and agency costs. The underlying notion is that of a leveraging parameter generated by co-financing of investment in the system. Our paper takes the argument a step forward by enabling the parameter to switch from positive to negative, thereby creating a 'crisis' of the kind observed intermittently in many parts of the world. The model also makes the parameter time varying by incorporating a feedback mechanism for production and investment decisions of the economy.

An explanation for the evolution dynamics leading to low and negative values of the FLC is the observation that falling levels of investment in the private sector and a slowdown in economic growth usually elicit demands for increased public investment, provision of guarantees to boost private investment, etc., consequently resulting in lower effectiveness of marginal investment.[10] An implication

---

10 An alternative explanation of the diminishing efficiency of investment might be the falling marginal productivity of capital (á

is that financial capital is not deployed productively; investment efficiency is thereby compromised. In other words, capital is increasingly deployed in unproductive (and ultimately in negative value) economic activity (in both public and private domains), i.e., where the value of inputs is more than the value of output due to forbearance in closing down ailing firms.[11] This is the intuition for growth to not only falter, but also turn negative. Note that in Eqn. (10), the sign of $\omega^*(t)$ depends on the ratio $\iota(t)/k(t)$ (= $(1-z(t))$). For large $\iota(t)/k(t)$, i.e., situations where the loan component to total investment is high, a smaller value of θ, an indicator of AMH, is sufficient to switch the leveraging coefficient. In other words, the more leveraged the system, the lower the threshold density required to switch to a decelerator.

Next, a switching mechanism for the FLC has to be incorporated. A simple specification is that $\omega^*(t)$ is a stochastic variable dependent on $\gamma(t)$. A possible behavioural specification for $\gamma(t)$ can be as follows:

$$\gamma(t) = E_{t-1}\, \gamma(t-1) + f(\varphi(\alpha(t))\, k(t)) + e(t) \qquad (11)$$

There are two sources of the stochasticity in the above specification of $\gamma(t)$: one is an endogenous source of uncertainty, arising from the stochastic productivity of capital $\alpha(t)$. This specification

---

la efficiency wage units) with the consequent interpretation of the FLC as a 'productivity efficiency' unit.

11 This diminishing efficiency of investment is accompanied by an increasing riskiness of the asset portfolio. Total capital-at-risk of a project can be decomposed into that of the sponsor (equity capital-at-risk) and of the lender (loan capital-at-risk). As a result of government-influenced intermediation, the nominal co-financing brought in by sponsors is allowed by the lender to be diluted, thereby lowering effective co-financing.

incorporates a simple feedback mechanism from the production side of the economy. However, there is also an inherent degree of uncertainty, arising exogenously, from the policies and behaviour of the government itself:[12] the possibility and extent of government bailouts of financially insolvent intermediaries.[13] This uncertainty is captured as an independent and uncorrelated error term, $e(t)$. $\gamma(t)$ is thus the key transmission mechanism for propagation of shocks across the real and financial sectors.

The probabilistic specification of $\gamma(t)$ and $\alpha(t)$ facilitates the formal introduction of two key notions in the paper: *hysteresis of government involvement* and *cascading moral hazard* in the financial sector. To reiterate, the basis underlying the hypothesized link between the real and financial sectors is that government involvement weakens the mechanisms normally used for mitigating moral hazard.

Hysteresis of government involvement arises from a stickiness built into the evolution equation of $\gamma(t)$. The rationale is that, in good times (state 1), there is little incentive for the government to change the status quo. In bad times (state 0), due to deepening financial distress, the government institutes measures that increase its involvement, viz., higher public sector investment levels, government guarantees and even government financing to 'jump-start' private capital formation, etc. Therefore, there is a systematic bias built into the movement of $\gamma(t)$, a component that has an

---

12 There is a growing body of literature on the institutional influences and political economy of the growth process and business cycles (see, for example, Alessina and Perotti [1994]).

13 The notion of 'destructive unambiguity' postulated by Mohanty and Patel (2000) has been modified; it has been replaced with a limited extent of uncertainty.

expected positive value. The other random component, with an expected value of zero, may lower the value of $\gamma(t)$ periodically (relative to the increasing trend), but has no systematic influence.

A 'cascading' moral hazard, which is the driving mechanism for the switch of the leverage coefficient, $\omega^*(t)$, from an accelerator to a decelerator, arises from this hysteresis and introduces a dynamic component to the concept of aggravated moral hazard introduced earlier. In other words, the aggravation is systematically augmented through the increasing government involvement, gradually weakening the mechanisms normally used to mitigate moral hazard such as higher requirements of capital, proper risk weighting, project monitoring, etc. Already low levels of notional co-financing are made even more ineffective. A continued weakening causes an eventual regime change when the leverage coefficient switches endogenously[14] from an accelerator to a decelerator, thereby bringing capital formation to a halt. An ancillary mechanism for the augmentation is the build-up of increasingly riskier portfolios through higher regulatory forbearance of closure of insolvent intermediaries that are publicly owned.

A simple mechanism to incorporate these concepts, drawing upon, among others, Hamilton's [1989] analysis of unobserved structural 'turning points', is to postulate the following difference equation for the driving process of $\gamma(t)$ specified in Eqn. (11): that it follows a Markov Trend in levels,

$$\gamma(t) = \gamma(t-1) + b\,(1 - \alpha(t))\,k(t) + e(t) \tag{12}$$

where $\alpha(t)$ can take on two values, 0 and 1, corresponding to the low and high state, respectively, of the system. In the high state,

---

14 In the sense that it is (partially) driven by the capital formation and production processes of the system.

γ(t) remains the same as before (except with uncorrelated random shocks, e(t)). If $\alpha(t) = 0$, there is an impact bk(t) on γ(t), which then feeds into γ(t+1) through the auto-regressive component in Eqn. (12). This incorporates an element of hysteresis in the behaviour of the 'density' parameter (see Figure A1.4).

Figure A1.4: Behaviour of γ(t) Showing Cascading and Hysteresis

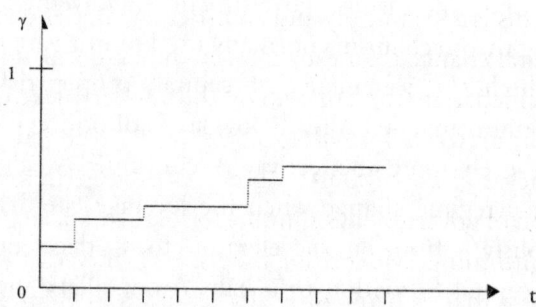

The transition between the states is governed by a first-order Markov process:

$$\Pr[\alpha(t) = 1 \mid \alpha(t-1) = 1] = p, \quad (13)$$

$$\Pr[\alpha(t) = 0 \mid \alpha(t-1) = 1] = 1 - p,$$

$$\Pr[\alpha(t) = 0 \mid \alpha(t-1) = 0] = q, \quad \text{and}$$

$$\Pr[\alpha(t) = 1 \mid \alpha(t-1) = 0] = 1 - q.$$

The above transition structure, together with the equation of motion of γ(t), implies

$$\alpha(t) = (1 - q) + \lambda\, \alpha(t-1) + v(t) \quad (14)$$

where $\lambda = p + q - 1$;

and $v(t)$ has the properties that although it is uncorrelated with the lagged values of $\alpha(t)$, viz.,

$E[v(t) \mid \alpha(t-1) = 0] = E[v(t) \mid \alpha(t-1) = 1] = 0$,

it is not independent of the lagged values of $\alpha(t)$, i.e.,

$E[v(t) \mid \alpha(t-1) = 0] = q(1 - q)$ and

$E[v(t) \mid \alpha(t-1) = 1] = p(1 - p)$.

In other words, the threshold is a structural event that is endogenous to the process of capital formation (and output) of the system. This is a technically and empirically a better characterization of structural change than exogenously imposed 'turning points'.

As a sidebar in the context of the model presented above, it also incorporates a formal mechanism to reconcile the curious discrepancy that is occasionally observed between the extensively held perception of government's support to some financial intermediaries (given continuing evidence of the asset quality of their portfolios being worse than is being officially reported even after an in-depth asset recognition exercise) being the sole prop preventing them from collapse, and publicly available data not indicating signs of an imminent financial crisis. This absence of explicit danger signals is captured by the unobserved component, $e(t)$, of the driving mechanism for $\gamma(t)$ in Eqn. (12) above. The government might be taking steps, like infusing capital in intermediaries and occasional reductions in the amount of resources directly intermediated, that are transitory in nature (and illusory) and serve to reduce the observed level of government involvement below their true levels. In other words, these transient actions serve to mask the event of true levels of involvement having crossed the threshold level and that the economy might already be in the 'collapse' state even while investment is still positive, though declining.

Proofs

Lemma:

$z^*(t) = [k(t) - \mu(t)\iota(t)] / k(t) = \{[k(t) - \iota(t)] / k(t)\} - \{(\mu(t) - 1) \iota(t) / k(t)\}$

$= z(t) - \beta(t)$

where $\beta(t) \equiv z^*(t) - z(t) = (\mu(t) - 1) \iota(t) / k(t) \geq 0$, since $\mu \geq 1$, by definition.

Proposition:

From Eqn. (10),

$\omega^*(t) = 1 + [z(t) + \{(1 - \mu(t)) (\iota(t) / k(t))\}]^{(-1)}$

$\omega^*(t) = 0 \Rightarrow [z(t) + \{(1 - \mu(t)) (\iota(t) / k(t))\}] = -1$ \hfill (A1.1)

Using the specification of $\mu(t)$ in Eqn. (7), and noting that $(\iota(t) / k(t)) = (1 - z(t))$, Eqn. (A2.1) can be rewritten as

$1 - \theta\Gamma^{(t)} = (-1) [1 + z(t)][1 - z(t)]^{(-1)}$

$\Rightarrow \theta\Gamma^{(t)} = 2 [1 - z(t)]^{(-1)}$

$\Rightarrow \Gamma(t) = \{\ln 2 - \ln[1 - z(t)]\} / \ln(\theta)$. \hfill (A1.2)

Existence of the solution, from Eqn. (A1.2) above, is ensured with a switch between a positive and a negative value of ω^* for some values of γ and the imposition of suitable restrictions on the values of θ that ensure that Γ is between 0 and 1.

Note that in the expression in square brackets on the right-hand side of Eqn. (10), $z(t)$ is positive and less than one and the multiplicative expression in curly brackets is less than or equal to zero. Therefore, given any particular level of $\iota(t)$ and $k(t)$, and assuming that the function in Eqn. (10) is continuous and differentiable, there exists a value of $\mu(t)$ where $\omega^*(t) = 0$.

As can be seen from expression (A1.2) above, the numerator consists of two expressions, both of which are negative. Given that z is less than 1, the absolute value of $\ln(1-z)$ is smaller than the absolute value of $\ln 2$, implying that the numerator is negative. For Γ to be positive, the denominator, i.e., $\ln(\theta)$, has to be negative. For Γ to be less than 1, $\ln(\theta) > \ln 2 - \ln[1 - z(t)]$.

Uniqueness of this solution requires appropriate constraints on the magnitudes of the parameters on the right side of Eqn. (10). The value of θ can be narrowed through a set of restrictions on this solution that ensures existence and uniqueness as well as congruence with the postulated theoretical properties of parameters.

Uniqueness is ensured if ω^* is downward sloping throughout the relevant range. This will be ensured if θ is less than a number which is less than the value of the natural exponent, e, i.e., 2.718, as shown below.

Differentiating Eqn. (10) w.r.t. γ,

$d\omega^* / d\gamma = (-1)[z + \{(1 - \theta^\gamma)(\iota / k)\}]^{(-2)} [\{(-1)(\iota/k)\} \{d(\theta^\gamma) / d\gamma\}] = \{(\iota / k)[z + \{(1 - \theta^\gamma)(\iota / k)]^{(-2)}\} \{d(\theta^\gamma) / d\gamma\}$ (A1.3a)

$d(\theta^\gamma) / d\gamma = \theta^\gamma \ln \theta$ (A1.3b)

The expression in the first curly brackets in A1.3a is positive. For $(d\omega^* / d\gamma) < 0$, for all values of γ, θ has to be less than that value where $\ln \theta = 0$.

The curvature of the function depends on the second derivative of ω^*. Differentiating Eqn. (A1.3a) again,

$d^2\omega^* / d\gamma^2 = (-1)(\iota/k)(\ln\theta)[\{z + \{(1 - \theta^\gamma)(\iota/k)\}\}^{(-2)} \{d(\theta^\gamma)/d\gamma\}]$

$+ 2\theta^\gamma (\iota/k) [\{z + \{(1 - \theta^\gamma)(\iota/k)\}\}^{(-3)} \{d(\theta^\gamma)/d\gamma\}\{d(\theta^\gamma)/d\gamma\}]$

$= (-1)\{(\iota/k)\theta(\ln\theta)^2\}[\{z + \{(1 - \theta^\gamma)(\iota/k)\}\}^{(-2)}$

$+ 2\theta^\gamma (\iota/k)\{z + \{(1 - \theta^\gamma)(\iota/k)\}\}^{(-3)}]$

Substituting $(\iota / k) = (1-z)$ in the above expression,

$d^2\omega^* / d\gamma^2 = (-1)\{(1 - z)\theta(\ln\theta)^2\}\{z + \{(1 - \theta^\gamma)(1 - z)\}\}^{(-2)}$

$$[1 + 2\theta^\gamma(1-z)\{1 - \theta^\gamma(1-z)\}^{(-1)}] \quad (A1.4)$$

The set of terms in the first two curly brackets are positive. The sign of the set of terms in the third curly brackets depends on the sign of $(1 - \theta^\gamma)$. This term can be simplified as follows:

$$1 + 2\theta^\gamma(1-z)\{1 - \theta^\gamma(1-z)\}^{(-1)} = \{1 + \theta^\gamma(1-z)\} / \{1 - \theta^\gamma(1-z)\}$$

When $\theta = 1$, the RHS becomes $(2-z)/z$, and expression (A1.4) becomes

$$d^2\omega^* / d\gamma^2 \big|_{\theta=1} = (-1)\{(1-z)(\ln 1)^2\}\{z\}^{(-2)} \{(2-z)/z\} < 0.$$

References

Alessina, and R. Perotti, 'The political economy of growth: A critical survey of the recent literature', *World Bank Economic Review*, vol. 8(3), 1994, pp. 351-371.

B. Bernanke and M. Gertler, 'Agency costs, net worth and business fluctuations', *American Economic Review*, vol. 79, 1989, pp. 257-276.

Bernanke, M. Gertler and S. Gilchrist, 'The financial accelerator and the flight to quality', NBER Working Paper No. 4789, 1994.

Bernanke, M. Gertler and S. Gilchrist, 'The financial accelerator in a quantitative business cycle framework', in J. B. Taylor and M. Woodford (Eds.) *Handbook of Macroeconomics*, Volume 1, Elsevier Science B.V., 1999.

J. D. Hamilton, 'A new approach to the economic analysis of nonstationary time series and the business cycle', *Econometrica*, vol. 57(2), 1989, pp. 357–384.

N. Mohanty and U. R. Patel, 'Moving ahead with financial sector reform', Mimeo., Infrastructure Development Finance Company Ltd., Mumbai, 2000.

R. Dekle and K. Kletzer, 'Domestic bank regulation and financial crises: Theory and empirical evidence from East Asia', NBER Working Paper No. 8322, 2001.

Appendix 2

PING-PONG: TIMELINE OF A LITIGATION (NCLT, NCLAT AND THE SC)

Round 1

1. In June 2017 – Bank 1 and Bank 2 filed Section 7 under the Insolvency and Bankruptcy Code, 2016, (IBC) against Defaulter before the National Company Law Tribunal (NCLT);
2. In August 2017 – The NCLT admitted the petitions filed by Bank 1 and Bank 2 under Section 7 of IBC;
3. In March 2018 – Resolution plans submitted by Bidder 1 and another by Bidder 2 were rejected by Resolution Professional (RP), on account of being ineligible under Section 29A, IBC;

4. In April 2018 – NCLT remanded the matter to the Committee of Creditors (CoC) for re-examination of the bids by Bidder 1 and Bidder 2;
5. In September 2018 – In the Appeal filed against the order of April 2018 of NCLT, the National Company Appellate Tribunal (NCLAT) allowed the resolution plan submitted by Bidder 2. Further, Bidder 1 was given time of three days to make payment of all overdue amounts with interest and charges in respect of non-performing accounts of two entities. In case Bidder 1 complied with the condition of payment of overdues, then CoC would consider the resolution plan by Bidder 1 along with the plan submitted by Bidder 2;
6. In October 2018 – In Appeal filed against the order of September 2018 of NCLAT, the Hon'ble Supreme Court held that both the bidders, i.e., Bidder 1 and Bidder 2, were ineligible under Section 29A of IBC. However, invoking Article 142 of the Constitution of India, the Hon'ble Supreme Court ruled that if the payments mandated under Section 29A are made by Bidder 1 and Bidder 2 within 2 weeks from the date of the judgment, in such event, bids submitted by all the eligible bidders (i.e., Bidder 1, Bidder 2 and Bidder 3) in the second round of bidding can be reconsidered by the CoC within the next eight weeks. In the event that no resolution plan is found worthy of acceptance by the requisite majority of the CoC, Defaulter would be liquidated.

Round 2

7. In March 2019 – NCLT conditionally allowed the resolution plan submitted by Bidder 1, and suggested that the

distribution of amounts amongst the financial creditors and operational creditors should be done in a fair and reasonable manner while making certain other observations.
8. In March 2019 – In the Appeal filed against the order of March 2019 of NCLT, the NCLAT directed that the resolution plan of Bidder 1 be implemented subject to decision of the NCLAT after considering the question of distribution between the financial creditors and the operational creditors.
9. In April 2019 – In the Appeal filed against the interim-order of March 2019 of NCLAT, the Hon'ble Supreme Court while hearing the challenge to the NCLAT order dated March 2019 directed that during the pendency of Appeal before NCLAT, the order of NCLT shall not be acted upon. Further, the Hon'ble Supreme Court also directed the NCLAT to hear the Appeal and pass its order expeditiously.

Round 3

10. In July 2019 – The NCLAT held that:
    - there can be no difference between the financial creditor and operational creditor in the matter of payment of dues and they deserve equal treatment under a resolution plan;
    - the profits generated by the Corporate Debtor during corporate insolvency resolution process would be distributed equally amongst the financial creditors and operational creditors;
    - the CoC has not been empowered to decide the manner in which distribution is to be made amongst the financial and operational creditors, as there would be conflict of interest between them.

11. In November 2019 – In Appeal filed against the order of July 2019 of NCLAT, the Hon'ble Supreme Court held that:
    - equitable treatment is to be given to each creditor depending upon the class to which it belongs, i.e., secured or unsecured, financial or operational;
    - NCLAT and NCLT cannot interfere with the decision of the CoC provided that it is in conformity with the provisions of the Code and the Regulations;

CoC has the freedom to classify and pay the secured creditors the amount, basis the value of their security, which they would have realized outside the process under the Code.

INDEX

aam aadmi depositors, 25
accounting standards, 137, 139, 156
advanced economies (AEs), 141
advance capital provisioning, 21
aggravated moral hazard (AMH), 8n11, 9, 44
agrarian economy, 112
agriculture, 86, 111, 112, 114, 116
    bank credit growth of, 112
    blanket relief to farmers, 117
    credit, 111–23
    crop insurance, 122
    eNAM, 123
    interest subvention scheme, 114
    kisan credit card, 114
    credit to landless farmers, 116
    Paramparagat Krishi Vikas Yojana, 123
    Pradhan Mantri Fasal Bima Yojana, 123
    Pradhan Mantri Krishi Sinchai Yojana, 123
agricultural debt relief, pros and cons of, 121
Aiyar, Swaminathan A., 71
Akerlof, George, 150
alphabet soup, 39, 51
Arab Monetary Fund, 145
artificial support to stock markets, 4

INDEX

asset classification, 18, 62–63
asset management companies, 54, 87
Asset Quality Review (AQR), 37–38, 44, 87, 90, 95
asset viability, 64
asymmetry of information, 14, 37

back-of-the-envelope calculation, 30, 57, 87
backward-looking prudential norms, 8
backward-looking regulation, 140
bad bank, 41–42
bad debts, 38, 71, 153
bailouts, 9, 26, 143
balance sheet, 4, 9, 26, 38, 41, 44, 49, 52, 56, 69, 73, 85, 114, 121, 155
bank credit–GDP ratio, 13, 112
Banking Companies (Acquisition and Transfer of Undertakings) Act, 1970, 7n9, 98
banking fraud, 30, 101, 102, 105
banking regulation, 9, 155
Banking Regulation (Amendment) Act, 2017, 48, 61, 74
Banking Regulation (BR) Act of 1949, 75, 98
banking regulator
    fraud prevention, 104–7
    powers, 36, 100–107

banking sector recapitalization, 54–55
bank nationalization, 3n1, 102
Bank Nationalization Act, 1980, 7n9, 98
bankruptcy, 8, 138, 156
banks' portfolio, sensitive component of, 49
bank-wise exposures, 36
Basel Committee on Banking Supervision, 142
Basel Core Principles (BCP), 96
Basel III requirement/commitment, 156
BCP (Basel Core Principles), 96
Becker, Gary, 126–34
behavioural change, 81
big data analytics, 140
books of accounts, 49
borrower-wise exposures, 36
BRICS countries, 145

CAG (Comptroller and Auditor General), 21
camel's nose under the tent, 91
capital deepening, 17, 112
capital flow management (CFM), 144, 146
capital to risk-weighted assets ratio (CRAR), 92
career-based rewards, 134
case-by-case approach, 75–76
cash flows, lack of continuous monitoring, 106

Index

cash profits, 106
Central Bureau of Investigation (CBI), 22, 99n10
central fraud registry, 103
Central Repository of Information on Large Credits (CRILC), 23n8, 36–37
Central Vigilance Commission (CVC), 22, 99n10, 125n2
CFM (capital flow management), 144, 146
Chekhov's gun, 159
CIRP (corporate insolvency resolution process), 66
cloud computing, 140
co-financing decline, 6
cognitive capture, 154
collateral damage, 121
commercial banks, 24, 36n2, 57, 98, 106
    credit information to CRILC, 57
    frauds trends, 106
    regulated by RBI, 98
    scheduled, 36
    state-controlled, 24
Committee of Creditors, 51
Comptroller and Auditor General (CAG), 22
Constitution of India
    Article 19(1)(g), 79
    Article 142, 186
cooperative banks, 13, 103n11
cooperative federalism, 149

corporate bonds outstanding, 13
corporate debt restructuring, 21, 63
corporate governance, 97–98, 137, 139
corporate insolvency resolution process (CIRP), 66
corporate litigants, 80
corporate-loan-related fraud, 106
coverage ratio, 49, 85, 92, 153
credit-binge 'party', 20
credit bubbles, 142
credit budgets, 4, 24
credit cycle, 7, 14, 139
credit enhancement, 152
credit-related cheating, 30
credit-worthy (corporate) borrowers, 9
Crime and Punishment, 126–34
CRISIL Ratings, 62
crisis formations, 149
crisis incidence, suddenness of, 140–41
crony capitalism, 65, 157
crop loans, short-term, 114–15
cross-border banking flows, 136
cross-sectional data, 150
currency management, 150

debt outstanding, 57
debt recovery tribunal (DRT), 81
debt-servicing, 81, 115
    capability, 22
    capacity, 14

INDEX

obligations, 22
payment, 76
Deposit Insurance and Credit Guarantee Corporation (DICGC), 103n11
destructive unambiguity, 9
detailed assessment report (DAR), 96
detection and punishment by the regulator, 100
detective vigilance, 125, 128–32, 134
Dharani Sugars case, 74
digital transactions, 150
disclosure, 49, 141–42
discriminatory Central bank swap, 143–46
downward-sticky deposit rates, 10
drum-beating higher credit growth, 7
due diligence, 6, 19, 20

ease of doing business, 66
ease of doing ranking, 90
e-commerce, 150
economic consequences, 81
economic incentives, 126–27
economic slowdown, 7, 25, 159
economic theory of incentives, 125
efficient procurement, 130
emerging market economies (EMEs), 137, 139, 141, 143–45

enforcement action, 52
enforcement of contracts, 66, 90
enforcement rules, 137
enhancement of collateral, 21
Eurasian Fund for Stabilization and Development, 145
evolving regulatory framework, 50–51
exposure threshold, 64
extant broad economic slowdown, 153
external auditor, 97
externality-agnostic objectives, 80

farm loan waivers, 8, 111, 117, 122
    brief history, 117
    budgetary provisions, 121
    first impact of, 121
    first major waiver, 1990, 117
    second waiver (2008), 117
    total cost of, 117
financial crisis, 141, 144, 150
financial inclusion, 123, 151
financialization, 135–46
Financial Resolution and Deposit Insurance (FRDI), 53-54, 156
Financial Sector Assessment Programme (FSAP), 94, 96–97
financial service provider (FSP), 156

Index

financial stability, 53, 74, 86, 100, 136, 139–40, 143–45, 149, 156
Financial Stability and Development Council (FSDC), 36–37
financial stability report (FSR), 26, 32, 83, 103, 105, 153
Financial System Stability Assessment (FSSA) report, 94
fiscal commitment, 86
fiscal deficit, 6, 122, 152
fiscalization, 3, 7
fiscal responsibility and budget management (FRBM), 57
fiscal space, 4, 11, 57–58
foreign portfolio investors, 26
forward-looking regulations, 61, 140
framework for revitalizing distressed assets, 38
frauds
  loan share of, 106
  powerful mechanisms against, 100
  prevention, 104–7
  quantum of, 32
  volume of, 106
fraudulent activity, 100

G20, 6
global external liabilities, 135
global financial crisis, 14, 136, 144, 146, 149, 156
global financial safety nets, inadequacy of, 143–46
global financial turbulence, 145
globalization and global rules/standards, 137–39
Gordian knot, 47
government banks (GB), 7, 17, 20, 22, 24–26, 30, 32, 38, 53–57, 59, 69, 82, 86–88, 90–91, 93, 96, 98–99, 101–3, 105, 107, 152, 154–56, 159
  corporate governance at, 98
  cost of risk capital for, 155
  cost per employee, 30
  day-to-day operational risk, 30
  decline in GNPAs of, 85
  decline in share of, 155
  divestment by joint ventures, 87
  equity investment in, 155
  exemptions for, 102
  flow of funds, 88
  giant employer, 25
  GNPA ratio for, 85n2, 87
  government's stake in, 55
  high cost structure of, 30
  inability to identify poor performing assets, 20
  increase in disclosed NPAs for, 38
  licence from RBI, 99
  market discipline mechanism for, 101
  no material disparity, 25

INDEX

non-operating expenses ratio, 30
obligations of, 57
outcome-agnostic incentives of, 80
periodic sector-wide salary adjustment, 25
vs private banks, 26, 30, 103
vs public banks, 30
recapitalization plan, 53, 105
share in the banking sector, 91
shrinking autonomy of, 86
guideline-based decision, 52

haircuts, 56, 82
high lending rates, 5
housing finance companies (HFCs), 13, 90
hyper-active regulatory environment, 141

IDBI Bank, 98
increasing capital requirements, 18
independence of the RBI, 96
Indian Banks Association (IBA), 39, 62, 77
inflation measured by the GDP, 112
information asymmetry, 36, 140
information deficit, 151
information technology protocol, 37
initiation of insolvency, 74, 76
insolvency, 41, 48, 51, 61, 73–74, 76, 81, 85, 143, 156
Insolvency and Bankruptcy Code (IBC), 39, 42–44, 48–49, 51, 56, 61–65, 71–80, 85–86, 91, 107, 154, 156–57
  compulsory reference to, 76
  credibility of, 78, 156
  insolvency process, 51
  intention of, 61
  RBI's revised framework, 65
  time limit of 180 days, 43
institutionalized fiscal rules, 138
inter-credit agreement (ICA), 76, 78, 82
Interest Subvention Scheme, 114–15
Internal Advisory Committee (IAC), 51, 61, 72, 76
Internal Audit Departments, 95
internal rating-based risk assessment, 141–42
international capital flows, 136
International Financial Reporting Standards (IFRS), 139, 156
International Monetary Fund (IMF), 26, 94, 105, 144, 146
investigative/vigilance/legal deterrence, 100

Jan Dhan Yojana, 25
Joint Lenders' Forum (JLF), 39–40, 46, 48

Index

Joint Liability Groups of 'Bhoomi Heen Kisan' (landless farmers), 116

kisan credit card, 114. *See also* agriculture

Latin American Reserve Fund, 145
legal framework for resolution, 42–46
lending cycle/asset build-up, 14
Life Insurance Corporation, 55–56, 87–88, 155
liquidation, 43, 46, 51, 64, 66, 68, 72, 81–82, 92, 96, 99, 153
living-dead borrowers, 44, 154

macroeconomic management, 3
macroeconomic surveillance, 149
macro-prudential measures (MPMs), 144, 146
management effectiveness, 49
market-based exchange rate regimes, 137
market-determined haircuts, 50
market discipline, 100–1
market failure, 47
market perception, 90
micro, small and medium enterprises (MSMEs), 65, 72, 78, 86, 90, 92, 154
    loans, forbearance for, 70
Minsky, Hyman, 149

'Minsky' moment, 150
monetary indiscipline, 138
monetary stability, objectives of, 136
monitoring, 49, 71, 134
moral hazard, 8, 56, 137, 142–42
mother of all moral hazard, 42
Mudra scheme, 24
multi-country currency swap, 145
multi-pronged approach, 85

National Bank for Agriculture and Rural Development, 116
National Company Law Appellate Tribunal (NCLAT), 80, 86
National Company Law Tribunal (NCLT), 32, 42, 51, 61, 64, 66, 72, 74–77, 82, 86, 91
negative risk perception, 14
non-banking financial companies (NBFCs), 13, 19, 73, 75, 90, 154
non-banking financial intermediation, 150
non-food credit, 14
non-performing assets (NPAs), 7, 9, 10, 13, 14, 19, 20–22, 26, 30, 32, 36, 38, 44, 49, 51, 65, 69–70, 72, 78, 85, 87–88, 105–6, 152, 158
    advance capital provisioning, 21
    assets classified as, 65

INDEX

average recoveries of, 92
carry cost of, 22
effect of, 9
elephant in the room, 30
escalation cycle, 86
induced (financial) shocks, 9
ratio, 30, 92
size and nature of, 35

operational efficiency, 71
operational failure, 104
operationalization, 64
operational risk, 30, 100, 105
overseeing committee (OC), 39, 50

Paramparagat Krishi Vikas Yojana, 123
pivotal voting, incentive failures, 40
policy contradictions catch up, 4
political credit cycles, 7
poor quality assets, 21
Pradhan Mantri Fasal Bima Yojana, 123
Pradhan Mantri Krishi Sinchai Yojana, 123
predictable monetary policy, 138
preventive vigilance, 125, 129, 132
private banks
  cost per employee, 30
  entry of, 5

vs government banks, 25
level field playing, 96
market discipline, 91
regulation, 91
regulatory quality, 104
revenue per employee, 30
privatization of banks, 158
profitability of crop production, 114
promoter-bank relationship, 47
prompt corrective action (PCA), 66–69, 101
provision coverage ratio (PCR), 14, 85, 92
Public Sector Borrowing Requirement, 6
public sector debt (loans), 59
punch bowl, 14, 20
Punjab National Bank, 49

quasi fiscal drivers, 24
quasi-fiscal instruments, 8

rate-cutting cycle, 10n14
real-estate sector, 73
real sector, living dead borrowers, 154
recap bonds, 54–56, 152
recapitalization, 53, 70
Recovery of Debts Due to Banks and Financial Institutions Act, 1993, 43, 72
recovery percentage, 86
reform, 42, 44, 66, 87, 102, 149

fiscal federalism, 148
monetary policy, 148
regulation, two-tier structure of, 154
regulatory discipline, 100
regulatory empowerment, 75
regulatory forbearance, 154
regulatory framework, 141
regulatory labelling of SIFIs/SIBs, 143
regulatory structure, 39
reinforced resolution, 47, 49, 51
Reserve Bank of India (RBI), 10, 148
　data on banking frauds, 101
　follow-up action, 50–51
　legal powers to supervise GBs, 96
　operational autonomy, 96
　powers on corporate governance, 98–99
　prompt corrective action, 101–2
　raised the exposure limit, 19
　regulatory powers over GBs, 102
reset and ring fence, 60
residential housing loans, risk weight for, 18
resolution, 41–46
restructured standard assets, 51, 63
risk recognition, 137
risk-tolerance thresholds, 95

role of economists, 147–51
role of financial regulation, 136
rule-based steady-state process, 72

Scheme for Sustainable Structuring of Stressed Assets (S4A), 39, 50
Securitisation and Reconstruction of Financial Assets and Enforcement of Security Interest Act, 2002 (SARFAESI), 43, 72, 81
security perfection, lack of, 106
self-correcting processes, 9
self-insurance, 143–46
sensitivity analysis, 18
shoehorn regulation, 140
single-window, 43, 85
smoke-and-mirrors genre, 56
sovereign guarantee for all creditors of GBs, 101
special mention accounts (SMA), 23n8, 36n2, 63
Special Purpose Power Assets Bank (SPPAB), 41n1
stakeholders, 17, 154
standard asset provisioning, 18
State Bank of India (SBI), 56
SBI Act, 1955, 7n9, 98
strategic debt restructuring (SDR), 39–40
stressed assets, 38
　ratio of, 38

INDEX

resolution, 105–7
stress-test scenarios, 18
subsidy recipients, payment risk for, 7
Supervisory Program for Assessment of Risk and Capital (SPARC), 94
    risk-based supervision system, 95
SWIFT system, 49
systemic risk management, 49

tactical assets for macroeconomic management, 154
telecom loans, 49
time-bound
    bankruptcy, 8, 137
    route for resolution, 43
    threat of an insolvency, 81
time-compliant process, 65
Too-big-to-fail (TBTF), 142–43
transparency, 10, 39, 141–42

unconstrained discretion, 44
under-predict actual default rates, 142
underwriting, 6, 106, 134

uniform accounting standards, 139
Union Budget, 24, 115

vehicles and asset management companies, 54, 87
vigilance, 124–34
    conceptual framework, 127, 130
    definition, 125
    detective vigilance, 125, 127–32, 134
    dynamic considerations, 132–33
    negative externalities, 125
    preventive vigilance, 125, 127–29, 131–32, 134
    punitive vigilance, 125, 127–29, 131–34

working capital, 5
World Bank (WB), 94

zombie borrowers, 157
zombie firms, 153

3Cs, 22
9Rs, 9–10

ABOUT THE AUTHOR

Urjit R. Patel served as the twenty-fourth Governor of the Reserve Bank of India. During his tenure he was a director of the Bank for International Settlements and a member of the Advisory Board of the Financial Stability Institute. Before his governorship he was the Deputy Governor in charge of monetary policy; he chaired a committee on strengthening monetary policy. From 2013 to 2018 he was Principal/Deputy in the G-20 and BRICS Finance Ministers' and Central Bank Governors' groups. Earlier, he worked with Reliance Industries and Infrastructure Development Finance Company.

He began his career as an economist with the International Monetary Fund. He has been a Consultant to the Indian Ministry of Finance, and a Non-resident Senior Fellow of Brookings Institution, Washington, DC. Last year he was awarded the Wilbur Cross Medal by Yale University. He is Honorary Fellow, Linacre College, Oxford.